WestBow Press books may be ordered through booksellers or by contacting:

WestBow Press
A Division of Thomas Nelson & Zondervan
1663 Liberty Drive
Bloomington, IN 47403
www.westbowpress.com
844-714-3454

ISBN: 978-1-6642-9441-7 (sc)
ISBN: 978-1-6642-9442-4 (hc)
ISBN: 978-1-6642-9443-1 (e)

Library of Congress Control Number: 2023904326

Print information available on the last page.

WestBow Press rev. date: 03/14/2023

CONTENTS

ACKNOWLEDGMENTS

I express gratitude to God for His guidance in the course of drafting this book. Additionally, I extend accolades to my lovely wife, Stephanie; likewise to my daughter, Lequicha; my son, Zachary; and his wife, Aurelia, for their support.

PREFACE

One morning while sitting in my office at the Ellen G. White Research Center, located on the campus of Oakwood University, I took a sweeping glance at the pictures of the *Morning Star* steamboat and the pioneers who worked to fulfill the mission of educating Blacks in the Jim Crow South after the Civil War (1861–1865). My mind soon wondered off into the concept of how boats have been used to providentially move people and cargo from one port to another. Boats have, in fact, changed the trajectory of many people's lives. I thought of Noah's Ark and his family who had never experienced a deluge of water before. I reflected on Peter's fishing boat, where Jesus, the incarnated Son of God, and the fulfillment of prophecy in Genesis 3:15, used to fulfil His mission of setting the captives free. I also recounted the *Mayflower*, which gave many pilgrims a new start after leaving the Old World. And then, there is the merchants' slave ship, the *Desire*, one of many. Countless numbers of black and bronze people were packed like sardines in the hull of this craft and carried over perilous seas to finally set foot on lands far distanced from their African birthplace.

Could the planks of wood from those vessels speak, I'm sure they would repeat stories of woe, victory, and eventually liberation of those who fought to make the lives of others better and who dared to pass the torch on so that the promise of a bountiful future could be realized. This book not only recounts the reason for the building of five of the floating forms of transportation mentioned and their purpose but also tells the story of oppressed people who used boats to escape to freedom. It describes secular and biblical metaphors of boats that characterize elements of liberation, freedom, free will, emancipation, and salvation.

Additionally, this book sets a historical context about the early beginnings of America and its efforts to establish a more perfect union. It intertwines biblical principles about bondage with Ellen G. White's prophetic perspectives about the topic as well. The latter part of the book tells the story of the *Morning Star* steamboat. It points out the key players who were instrumental in reaching people of color after the Civil War and aligns the overall mission to the southern region of America with man's duty to reach all people in spreading the gospel, no matter what their race, creed, or color may be. The book also shares the legacy of important African Americans who played a significant role in spreading Adventism to Black America. It is this amazing story and the visual pictures of Edson White's steamboat, the *Morning Star*, on my office wall that inspired me to write this book.

INTRODUCTION

Freedom seekers have made countless voyages to the newfound land of America in search of freedom, liberty of conscience, and justice for all. Numerous pilgrims came voluntarily while others arrived as slaves and were coerced and shackled. Although according to Samuel Cartwright (1851) slaves were subhuman and the Constitution was not designed for them, Providence orchestrated that both cohorts were destined for freedom because America is dubbed "the land of the free." Freedom was codified in its Declaration of Independence, which stated in the preamble, "We hold these truths to be self-evident, that all men are created equal, that they are endowed by their Creator with certain unalienable Rights, that among these are Life, Liberty, and the pursuit of Happiness." The codification of freedom made it possible that although many people of color may have journeyed across the Atlantic Ocean in chains and suffered the negative effects of slavery, they would eventually be free. The casualties that the slaves experienced and the pilgrims encountered in quest to meet their objectives were collateral for the degree of liberty that we all are granted today. This is because freedom is not free; it often causes the ultimate price of life itself.

Authentic education about this nation's development is crucial to the perpetuation of liberty and the evolution of a more unified country. Providing an accurate historical account of America's initial challenges with ensuring equal rights for every citizen in the hope of raising awareness and catapulting the framers' ideals of democracy toward a more perfect union is vital to the well-being of each state in the union. The framers understood that the experiment of a republic and democratic union was imperfect and would need a continuation of assessing and modifying as it progresses toward its ideal. Unfortunately, since the election of the forty-fifth president in 2016, the fragility of the Constitution and its content has been revealed. We have seen that authenticity, truthfulness, and justice are necessary ingredients to sustain the republic.

The wayfarers who made treacherous voyages to the New World after attempts to reform the Old World were in search of more freedom and less government and papal control. They understood that by engaging in protest, religiopolitical entities that sought to enslave and oppress their free will would not be just a physical undertaking, but a spiritual conflict. They were Protestants who believed in liberty of conscience but were prohibited from exercising this gift of the Creator. Consequently, in 1519 AD, about 97 years before the Mayflower first docked in Massachusetts in search of liberty of conscience, Martin Luther the reformer stated, "My conscience is captive to the Word of God … Therefore, where temporal power presumes to prescribe laws for the soul it encroaches upon God's government and only misleads and destroys the souls" (Loconte 2017). Martin Luther's desire to correct systems that conflicted with Scripture, and his understanding of the rules of spiritual engagement were manifested in protest. Martin Luther understood from the grand biblical metanarrative that he was involved in a cosmic conflict between good and evil. He believed that maliciousness of evil can only be conquered by demonstration and active engagement.

In our spiritual melees against systems of evil, the questions that we must ask and answer are as follows: Who inspired concepts of religious intolerance, racial inferiority, casteism, oppression, and the establishment of political and social policies to perpetuate them? Is God responsible? Emphatically, no! Over a century ago, Ellen White (1913) explained, God is love, He takes no pleasure in a forced or deceived allegiance. To all created beings, He grants freedom of will, that they may render Him voluntary service. God desires from all His creatures the service of love—homage that springs from an intelligent appreciation of His character. However, there was one that chose to pervert this freedom. Evil originated with him who, next to Christ, had been most honored of God and who stood highest in power and glory among the inhabitants of heaven. Before his fall, Lucifer was first of the covering cherubs, holy and undefiled. "You were the seal of perfection, Full of wisdom and perfect in beauty. You were in Eden, the garden of God; Every precious stone was your covering: The sardius, topaz, and diamond, Beryl, onyx, and jasper, Sapphire, turquoise, and emerald with gold. The workmanship of your timbrels and pipes Was prepared for you on the day you were created. "You were the anointed cherub who covers; I established you; You were on the holy mountain of God; You walked back and forth in the midst of fiery stones. You were perfect in your ways from the day you were created, Till iniquity was found in you" (Ezekiel 28:12--15).

The manifestation of iniquity in Lucifer is the foundation of evil and the byproduct of dehumanizing policies, social discord, racial disharmony, and tyranny. All nefarious acts are consequences of iniquity, which had its origin with Lucifer when he violated God's law of love in heaven. Anyone who covertly or overtly practices and devises the abovementioned evils is not adhering to the Spirit of God but the spirit of Lucifer. The Bible says, "He was a murderer from the beginning, and does not stand in the truth, because there is no truth in him. When he speaks a lie, he speaks from his own resources: for he is a liar and the father of it" (John 8:32 NKJV). He incubated and birthed lies. The only way to expose the spirit of Lucifer is through truth telling about his influence on world leaders as they formulated oppressive systems of government in the course of history.

Critical race theory (CRT) reveals the truth about the spirit or being who conceals himself behind racism in America and the world. Luciferian spirits are directing those persons who attempted to conceal historical facts and truths by removing books from the library and perhaps even burning them as other despots in history did. They are in partnership with the enemy of freedom. Legal scholars who supported the preservation of democracy in the 1970s and 1980s formed CRT after the civil rights movement to disprove the idea that society and its laws are now just and colorblind. This contradicted the framers' ideal of the Constitution that it should progress toward a more perfect union. CRT is an academic and legal concept that points out the United States' constitutional breach and believes that systemic racism has become an integral part of America's society. This theory suggests that the evidence of racism manifested in disproportionate incarcerations among Blacks, unemployment disparities, preventable medical problems, unequal healthcare, miseducation, and police brutality.

Racism is not just a result of social biases and prejudices. It is a facet of the cosmic conflict between good and evil. It is intentionally embedded in politics, policies, laws, governmental, and financial systems that reinforce, reproduce, and perpetuate social disparities. An example is, during the 1930s, when government officials drew lines around communities that they considered to be high financial risks. This was explicitly due to racial composition of the people who lived there. Financial institutions refused to make mortgages to people of color in those areas. The same pattern of inequity in policies are manifested in single-family zoning that prevents building affordable housing in advantaged majority-white communities, thereby inhibiting desegregation efforts (Sawchuk 2021).

Higher mortality rates, overexposure to police violence, high rates of childbirth deaths among Black females, denial of affordable housing, and the school-to-prison pipeline are not unrelated anomalies. They can be traced to the violation of the Constitution that allows racist laws and policies that are now inherent in many institutions in the United States. Racism and eugenics, which many false cultural views are based, promote the idea that members of some races are subhuman. However, race is not a natural organic biologically founded characteristic of physically distinct subgroup of human beings but a socially constructed and culturally invented concept that society uses to oppress and exploit people of color (Sawchuk 2021).

Embracing the United States Constitution is an avenue to promote freedom and equality for all people. If it does not conflict with Scriptures, it is a tool for justice. However, we must be aware of the contemporary and increasingly popular judicial philosophy called originalism, which conflicts with the Bible because it seeks to interpret the Constitution by holding the intent and thoughts of the framers supreme. When originalist judges make legal decisions according to beliefs eighteenth-century white men, who denied a right to own property and vote to anyone except themselves, they are not progressing toward a more perfect union but regressing to a more disunified country by denying liberty and justice for all.

Five legendary boats will be used in this book as metaphors to chronicle and explain the root cause of the development of oppression and the passing of laws that perpetuated it. These boats, which played a pivotal role in God's providential discourse, charted the course of history and prophetic occurrences. Through each of them, the drama of the ages, or the cosmic conflict, is manifested in struggles for liberty

CHAPTER ONE

THE ARK

GOD'S MOTIVATION FOR THE ARK

One thousand six-hundred and fifty-six years after creation, the evil and disunity that Satan instigated in heaven were wreaking havoc on earth. He had deceived Adam and Eve and infected their offspring with the venom of sin (Genesis 1–6). "And God saw that the wickedness of man was great in the earth, and that every imagination of the thoughts of his heart was only evil continually. And it repented the LORD that he had made man on the earth, and it grieved him at his heart. And the LORD said, I will destroy man whom I have created from the face of the earth; both man, and beast, and the creeping thing, and the fowls of the air; for it repents me that I have made them" (Genesis 6:5–7). The ark was employed expressly to address the aggrandizement of wickedness in the earth and its oppressive effects on preceding generations. Every imagination of humans' thoughts was evil continually. The original Hebrew phrase for *continually* is סוֹם. It is pronounced "ha-yome," which means "uninterrupted wicked thoughts and behavior all day and every day." Evil, as a king, reigned supremely in the hearts, in the imagination, and in the actions of human beings. Humankind was completely sensual, the desires of their minds overwhelmed and lost in the desires of the flesh, their souls no longer discerning their high destiny, but ever minding earthly things until they were amalgamized and continually immersed in falsehood and the evil of their generation.

Amalgamation is a byproduct of egregious immorality. The Bible highlighted that amalgamation was a primary continual sin that was practiced before the flood: "And it came to pass, when men began to multiply on the face of the earth, and daughters were born unto them, that the sons of God saw the daughters of men that they were fair; and they took them wives of all which they chose" (Genesis 6:1–2 KJV). In commenting on this text, White (1945) stated, "But if there was one sin above another which called for the destruction of the race by the flood, it was the base crime of amalgamation of man and beast which defaced the image of God and caused confusion everywhere. God purposed to destroy by a flood that powerful, long-lived race that had corrupted their ways before him." She suggested that the wickedness of amalgamation prompted God to commission Noah to build an ark. God desired to save original species of animals and His faithful followers while destroying amalgamated forms of life. Nichol (1951) posited the following:

1. It was the "one sin above another which called for the destruction of the race by the Flood."

2. It "defaced the image of God and caused confusion everywhere."

3. "That powerful, long-lived race ... had corrupted their ways before him."

Two distinct groups of human beings are presented at the opening of the chapter in *Spiritual Gifts*, volume 3, entitled "Crime before the Flood": (1) "the descendants of Seth," and (2) "the descendants of Cain." The two groups were distinct in two marked ways: (1) the first group "felt the curse but lightly," and (2) the second group, "who turned from God and trampled upon his authority, felt the effects of the curse more heavily, especially in stature and nobleness of form." "The descendants of Seth were called the sons of God—the descendants of Cain, the sons of men." Here two races are presented that differ both in moral and physical characteristics.

Then follow immediately these words: "As the sons of God mingled with the sons of men, they became corrupt, and by intermarriage with them, lost, through the influence of their wives, their peculiar, holy character, and united with the sons of Cain in their idolatry." Next comes a description of their evil course of idolatry, particularly their prostituting to sinful ends the gold and silver and other material possessions that were theirs. Mrs. White then observes: "They corrupted themselves with those things which God had placed upon the earth for man's benefit." From a discussion of idolatry, she turns to polygamy and makes this statement: "The more men multiplied wives to themselves, the more they increased in wickedness and unhappiness" (pp. 60–63).

For a period of time the two classes of people remained separate. The race of Cain, spreading from the place of their first settlement, dispersed over the plains and valleys where the children of Seth had dwelled; and the latter, to escape from their contaminating influence, withdrew to the mountains, and there made their home. So long as this separation continued, they maintained the worship of God in its purity. But in the lapse of time, they ventured, little by little, to mingle with the inhabitants of the valleys. This association was productive of the worst results. "The sons of God saw the daughters of men that they were fair." The children of Seth, attracted by the beauty of the daughters of Cain's descendants, displeased the Lord by intermarrying with them. Many of the worshippers of God were beguiled into sin by the allurements that were now constantly before them, and they lost their peculiar, holy character. Mingling with the depraved, they became like them in spirit and in deeds; the restrictions of the seventh commandment, "Thou shalt not commit adultery," were disregarded, "and they took them wives of all which they chose." The children of Seth went "in the way of Cain"; they fixed their minds upon worldly prosperity and enjoyment and neglected the commandments of the Lord. Therefore, God's motivation for the ark was to eliminate the continued evil practice of amalgamation of humans and beasts from the earth. Amalgamated DNA transmitted intergenerationally caused God's people to be predisposed and enslaved to the murderous tendencies of Cain (White, 1890). Thus, the ark was built!

THE CONFIGURATION OF THE ARK

To minimize the contagious effects of amalgamation God admonished Noah, "Make you an ark of gopher wood; rooms shall you make in the ark and shall pitch it within and without with pitch. And this is the fashion which you shall make it of: The length of the ark shall be three hundred cubits, the breadth of it fifty cubits, and the height of it thirty cubits. A window shall you make to the ark, and in a cubit shall you finish it above; and the door of the ark shall you set in the side thereof; with lower, second, and third stories shall you make it" (Genesis 6:14–16).

God gave Noah the precise dimensions of the ark and explicit directions regarding its construction in every aspect. In many respects, it was not made like a sea vessel but prepared like a house with rooms and cells, which literally means "nests" that were especially for the many animals. The word translated *pitch* is of Babylonian origin and is also translated bitumen, which is a form of petroleum, sticky, black, and highly viscous liquid like molasses that becomes semisolid and eventually totally solidified. Since ancient times, such materials have been found in Mesopotamia and were used for caulking ships (White,1945).

The base of the ark was constructed as the hull of a ship, but the rudimentary design was like that of a house with three floors, one side door, and windows. The first window is referred to in Genesis 6:16 as the tsohar and is said to be one cubit (1.5 feet) from the top of the boat. It is described as a skylight, giving light to those living inside of the edifice. It was a marvelous creation, and seemingly unknown to humankind of that day.

The ark had two additional openings. The second is denoted as the *jallón* (Genesis 8:6). Unlike the third window, the *jeseh* (Genesis 8:3), which Noah used to examine the surface of the land, the jallón was opened by Noah when he released the raven and the dove to determine whether the floodwaters had subsided. Noah closed the jallón when the birds returned to the ark. This window was probably located in the area where Noah's family lived. Windows could only be opened from the inside, and the entrance door could only be opened by an angel who shut the door eight days before the flood and opened it forty days later (White 1985, 1946).

However, the foundation was like a boat that would float upon water. There were no windows in the sides of the ark. It was three stories high, and the light they received was from a window in the top. The door was in the side. The different apartments prepared for the reception of different animals were so made that the window in the top gave light to all. The ark was made of the cypress or gopher wood, which would know nothing of decay for hundreds of years. It was a building of great durability that no wisdom of man could invent. God was the designer, and Noah his master builder.

The largest ancient vessel that can be compared to the ark was an Egyptian ship that was up to 130 cubits (195 feet) long and 40 cubits wide (60 feet). The ark of Noah was almost three times as long. The biblical cubit of 20.6 inches, as cited in Deuteronomy 3:11, suggests that the length of the ark would have been 515 feet, its width 86 feet, and its height 52 feet. A more contemporary comparison is a football field (360 feet long). The ark was over half the length of a football field and almost half as wide and had the form of a box or chest like the ark of the covenant that housed the commandments rather than a ship (SDA Bible Commentary vol. 1). This will be discussed later in this chapter.

SOTERIOLOGICAL IMPLICATIONS

Soteriology is a branch of theology that focuses on the nature and venue of salvation. It is taken from the Greek *soterion*, which literally means "deliverance." Chris Ashcraft embodied deliverance in his research that was posted on his website. He presented narratives from different flood accounts in various countries and their salvific and soteriological implications, which are as follows:

- East Africa
- Argentina

- Australia
- Bolivia
- Borneo
- Burma
- Cuba (original natives)
- Fiji
- Egypt (Book of the Dead)
- Iceland
- India
- Mexico
- New Zealand
- Russia-Vogul
- Vietnam-Bahnar

Out of the thirty-five flood stories that were examined, including the ones listed above, all of them talked of humans being saved from a flood. Thirty-two of them include a boat, twenty-four include an account of animals being saved. All these legends portrayed the boats used as vessels of safety and deliverance for people and animals (NW Creation Network 2022).

Strong's Concordance listed the original Hebrew word for *ark* as *tevah*, which appears in only two places in the Old Testament. The first place is Genesis chapter 6 where God directed Noah to prophesy and build an ark as a vehicle of salvation to endure the flood and save His people. The second place the ark is mentioned is Exodus chapter 2 when Moses's mother, Jachebed, built a flotation device from bulrushes and daubed it with slime and pitch and placed baby Moses in it. In both instances, the ark served as instruments of salvation. It was used for a sacred purpose, which was to provide a divine means of escape for infant Moses and salvation for God's chosen people.

According to an article in *National Geographic* by Than (2010), Noah's ark has been found adjacent the top of Mount Ararat in Turkey. The group of evangelical Christian excavators discovered the remains of the ark beneath the snow and volcanic debris. The team members said that they are 99.9 percent sure of their finding. According to Scripture, the ark rested on Mount Ararat after the flood (Than 2010). Whether this discovery is Noah's ark or not, the Bible clearly stated that the ark rested on Ararat.

However, the ark of the Covenant has different Hebrew words, *Aron Ha-Brit*, which literal English translation is synonymous with its name. It means "a chest, coffin, casket, or box." The ark of the Covenant is particularly mentioned in Exodus, Deuteronomy, and Joshua. The gold-covered acacia wood box measured 2.5 x 1.5 x 1.5 cubits and symbolized the presence of God. It served to protect sacred articles and artifacts of God. Although the words for *ark* differ in meaning, symbolically, both were designed to offer divine protection for God's people and the things of God (Elwell 1996).

According to the Bible the descendants of Adam, as stated in Genesis 3–8, had become increasingly engrossed and enslaved to sin since the fall. This grieved God, and He promised to liberate and save those who accepted the message sent through Noah but destroy those who rejected it. The Bible stated that "every imagination of the thoughts of his heart was only evil continually." They were held in spiritual captivity by sin. God became weary of them because their thoughts and behavior consisted only of sinful pleasure and indulgences. They did not seek the counsel of God, the One who had created them, nor cared to do his will. The rebuke of God was upon them because they followed the imaginations of their own selfish hearts. Kinlaw (2017) believed Satan disguises submission to himself under the ruse of personal autonomy. He never asks us to become his servants. Never once did the serpent say to Eve, "I want to be your master." The shift in commitment is never from Christ to evil; it is always from Christ to self.

Selfishness illustrated by God's people intermarrying heathen spouses and violence were in the land. "And it repented the Lord that he had made man on the earth, and it grieved him at his heart. ... And God looked upon the earth, and behold, it was corrupt; for all flesh had corrupted his way upon the earth. And God said unto Noah, the end of all flesh is come before me; for the earth is filled with violence through them; and behold, I will destroy them with the earth."

Symbolism

The ark typified salvation and is a symbol of free will because God cannot force us to accept Him. Tozer (2021) endeavors to reconcile the apparently paradoxical beliefs of God's sovereignty and humanity's free will in the following allegory:

> An ocean liner leaves New York bound for Liverpool. Its destination has been determined by proper authorities. Nothing can change it. This is at least a faint picture of sovereignty. On board the liner are scores of passengers. These are not in chains, neither are their activities determined for them by decree. They are completely free to move about as they will. They eat, play, lounge about on the deck, read, talk, altogether as they please; but all the while the great liner is carrying them steadily onward toward a predetermined port. Both freedom and sovereignty are present here, and they do not contradict. So it is, I believe, with man's

freedom and the sovereignty of God. The mighty liner
of God's sovereign design keeps its steady course over
the sea of history.

God's sovereign was seen in the inevitability of the flood.
Yet free will was illustrated by God's provision of the ark to save
everyone who chooses to get on board. God instructed Noah to
build a boat, the first of its kind, to liberate from destruction all
of those who desired to be saved. This is the same free will that
God gave the first couple, which prohibited Him from forcing
liberty and salvation on them. It also prevented Satan from coercing
the conscience. Additionally, it fixed the fight in our favor and
empowered humankind to freely choose their own destinies. That
means if we want to be saved, we can! All the demons in hell cannot
stop us. White (1963) explained:

> In the sentence pronounced on Satan in the garden,
> the Lord declared, "I will put enmity between thee
> and the woman, and between thy seed and her seed; it
> shall bruise thy head, and thou shalt bruise His heel."
> (Genesis 3:15). This was a promise that the power of
> the great adversary would finally be broken. Adam
> and Eve stood as criminals before the righteous Judge,
> but before they heard of the toil and sorrow which
> must be their portion or that they must return to dust,
> they listened to words that could not fail to give them
> hope. They could look forward to final victory. Satan
> knew that his work of depraving human nature would
> be interrupted, that by some means man would be
> enabled to resist his power (p. 333).

Free will was a major factor for those who would accept Noah's message of salvation and entered the ark. God placed humankind under law for their safety. God might have created us without the power to transgress; He might have withheld Adam from touching the forbidden fruit; but in that case, we would have been mere automatons. Without freedom of choice, our obedience would have been forced. Such a course would have been contrary to God's plan, unworthy of human beings as intelligent beings, and would have sustained Satan's charge of God's arbitrary rule (White 1984). The ark was symbolic of freedom of choice and illustrated that God is not arbitrary.

Perhaps there were other flotation devices and mechanisms that humans constructed in the pre-flood era. However, according to the Bible, the ark was the very first boat of its type ever built during human history that offered humans an alternative to the bondage of sin. Before the flood, rain had never fallen and threatened sinners' existences, and an ark or boat was not necessary. God designed the very first boat of its kind to be used to liberate mankind from sin and from death. Liberty is one of the primary themes of God. Because God is love, the very laws of His Kingdom is love, which is reflected in the Ten Commandments—love to God and love for humanity. Love fuels free will. Angels were created with free will. Lucifer understood free will because he himself was created with it. That's why he, while in heaven, was able to deceive angels, and Adam and Eve in the Garden of Eden could choose to sin.

Freedom that the gospel gives, and freedom of choice are guarded by God. In reference to Jesus's mission, Isaiah the prophet wrote, "The Spirit of the Lord God is upon me, Because the Lord has anointed me to bring good news to the afflicted; He has sent me to bind up the brokenhearted, to proclaim liberty to the captives and freedom to prisoners" (Isaiah 61:1 ESV). David declared, "Out of my destress

I called on the Lord; the Lord answered me and set me free" (Psalm 118:5 ESV). Jesus said, "Ye shall know the truth, and the truth shall make you free" (John 8:32 KJV).

PROPHETIC CONNOTATIONS

The ark had prophetic connotations in that the activities of humankind before the flood will characterize people living before the second advent. Jesus alluded to these events in the book of Mathew: "But as the days of Noah were, so shall also the coming of the Son of man be. For as in the days that were before the flood they were eating and drinking, marrying, and giving in marriage, until the day that Noah entered into the ark, And knew not until the flood came, and took them all away; so shall also the coming of the Son of man be" (Matthew 24:37–39).

Despite the warning presented by Noah and the testimony illustrated by the building of the ark, men and women went about their usual round of work and pleasure, utterly heedless of events soon to transpire. This same unconcern spirit will be portrayed by humankind in the days before Jesus's second coming. Their activities, too, as those of the antediluvians, would be evil continually. The sons of God intermarried unbelievers, practiced polygamy, and celebrated these unions by eating and drinking. The flood overtook them while they were engaged and preoccupied in their usual rounds of ungodly activities. The same will be true at the time of the second advent when the Spirit of God is withdrawn from the earth (Genesis 6:3) and a time of trouble ensues, allowing evil to run rampant before God eternally delivers His chosen ones from sin's grip (Daniel 12:1).

CHAPTER TWO

PETER'S FISHING BOAT

Over two thousand years after the flood, the progression of evil among humanity continued. God again was compassioned. Instead of sending another prophet to build a boat, He sent His only Son to be a vessel to rescue perishing humans and to be sin's antidote, thereby freeing them from demons that held them captive. White, 2002 wrote the following:

The deception of sin had reached its height. All the agencies for depraving the souls of men had been put in operation. The Son of God, looking upon the world, beheld suffering, and misery. With pity He saw how men had become victims of satanic cruelty. He looked with compassion upon those who were being corrupted, murdered, and lost. They had chosen a ruler who chained them to his car as captives. Bewildered and deceived, they were moving on in gloomy procession toward eternal ruin, —to death in which is no hope of life, toward night to which comes no morning. Satanic agencies were incorporated with men. The bodies of human beings, made for the dwelling place of God, had become the habitation of demons. The senses, the nerves, the passions, the organs of men, were worked by supernatural agencies in the indulgence of the vilest lust. The very stamp of demons was impressed upon the countenances of men. Human faces reflected the expression of the legions of evil with which they were possessed. Such was the prospect upon which the world's Redeemer looked. What a spectacle for Infinite Purity to behold!

Sin had become a science, and vice was consecrated as a part of religion. Rebellion had struck its roots deep into the heart, and the hostility of man was most violent against heaven. It was demonstrated before the universe that, apart from God, humanity could not be uplifted. A new element of life and power must be imparted by Him who made the world ... Satan was exulting that he had succeeded in debasing the image of God in humanity. Then Jesus came to restore in man the image of his Maker. None but Christ can fashion anew the character that has been ruined by sin. He came to expel the demons that had controlled the will. He came to lift us up from the dust, to reshape the marred character after the pattern of His divine character, and to make it beautiful with His own glory (p. 36, 37).

Jesus used numerous of methods of reaching humanity to save them from oppressive demonic spirits. These evil forces were operating through human instrumentalities from the kingdom of darkness. In Peter's time, he came personally. He took on Himself the garbs of humanity with all its limitations and risks to set us free. He availed himself of boats, which were the transportation that the average human being would use at that time. He particularly borrowed Peter's vessel to facilitate His purpose.

THE CONFIGURATION OF PETER'S BOAT

What did Peter's boat look like? Unlike Noah's ark, there is no description of Peter's boat in the New Testament. However, in 1985, a fishing boat from the first century was uncovered in the mud along the shore of the sea of Galilee. The water levels of the sea had been declining for several decades because of drought and overuse in the last century and were reaching their lowest level in a century. This decrease in water level allowed this boat to be discovered. Whether the boat belonged to one of Jesus's followers is not known. However, it does help us to understand what boats of that era looked like (Kasten 2018). According to the Yigal Allon Museum, the boat was 27 feet long,

7.5 feet wide, and about 4 feet deep. It was made of different types of wood but mostly cedar and oak that were pegged together. It was large enough to hold about fifteen people. That would include the capacity to board Jesus, the twelve disciples, plus three additional persons. The witness of this ancient Galilee fishing vessel reminds us that the Lord lived and worked among everyday working people, and it was these individuals He called to be disciples (Kasten 2018).

Hayes, John, Mandell, and Sara (1998) believed that the boat discovered in Galilee in the twentieth century can be dated back to the first century AD. They called it "the Jesus boat." It probably had a cutwater bowl and a recurving side. This vessel apparently represents the largest boat of its type that was used on lakes in antiquity. It was used primarily for fishing in the rich waters of the Sea of Galilee, although it may also have been used to transport passengers and supplies around and across the lake.

Hayes, John, Mandell, Sara (1998) also suggested that the vessel was built using the shell-based technique, in which the hull's planking was built up before so that the frame could be inserted. The planks were edged jointed by means of mortise-and-tenon joints.

This method of constructing boats is well known from Mediterranean shipwrecks dated as early as 1300 BC through the Roman period, until it was replaced by skeleton-based construction in the first millennium AD. Eminent ship reconstructor Professor J. Richard Steffy of the Institute of Nautical Archaeology at Texas A&M University, who studied the boat during its excavation, concluded that the techniques employed in its construction were consistent with those common on the Mediterranean around 100 BC through AD 200.

The boat builders either learned this trade on the Mediterranean or had been apprenticed to a Mediterranean shipwright. At first glance, the planking pattern and choice of timbers used in the hull appear strange. Some planks are unusually narrow, and frames are poorly fitted to hull curves. However, this may be the result of a shortage of affordable wood, which forced and expert shipwright to use inferior timbers that on the Mediterranean coast would have been discarded as unsuitable. The hull features numerous timbers that appears to have been recycled.

Pegged mortise-and-tenon joints were used to edge-joint the hull planks together, and iron nails were driven from the outside served to secure the frames to the hull. The boat had a fine bow and deep site. According to Dr. Ella Werker of the Department of Botany, Hebrew University, Jerusalem, the hole was constructed primarily of Lebanese cedar planks and oak frames, but ten other wood types have been documented in it. This may suggest that it could have been a wood shortage in which the boatwright was unable to secure appropriate timber, or perhaps the boat owner was too poor to afford it.

CHRISTOCENTRIC PURPOSE

Apostle Peter was a fisherman by trade, which means that his sailboat was vital to his business. Before meeting Jesus, he utilized it for economical purposes. After being called and commissioned by Jesus, it was repurposed and additionally used to fish for souls. One night after spending the entire night in his boat fishing without success, he and his brother Andrew folded their nets and came to shore with disappointed hopes. Jesus used their fruitless night on the lake to fulfill His prophetic role and teach an object lesson about how to liberate souls from sin's grip.

The crowds were very large and pressing upon Jesus, and He needed a better platform to teach and evangelize. So He requested from Peter to use his boat. The moment Jesus entered the boat, it was not the same. It was transformed from ordinary business usage to a holy purpose. It became a floating Sanctuary to save humans from their sin (Matthew 4:18–22; Mark 1:16–20; Luke 5:1–11). White (2002) explains:

> Day was breaking over the Sea of Galilee. The disciples, weary with a night of fruitless toil, were still in their fishing boats on the lake. Jesus had come to spend a quiet hour by the waterside. In the early morning He hoped for a little season of rest from the multitude that followed Him day after day. But soon the people began to gather about Him. Their numbers rapidly increased, so that He was pressed upon all sides. Meanwhile the disciples had come to land. In order to escape the pressure of the multitude, Jesus stepped into Peter's boat, and bade him pull out a little from the shore. Here Jesus could be better seen and heard by all, and from the boat He taught the multitude on the beach. What a scene was this for angels to contemplate; their glorious Commander, sitting in a fisherman's boat, swayed to and fro by the restless waves, and proclaiming the good news of salvation to the listening throng that were pressing down to the water's edge! He who was the Honored of heaven was declaring the great things of His kingdom in the open air, to the common people. Yet He could have had no more fitting scene for His labors. The lake, the mountains, the spreading fields, the sunlight flooding the earth, all furnished objects to illustrate His lessons and impress them upon the mind. And no lesson of Christ's fell fruitless. Every message

from His lips came to some soul as the word of eternal
life (p. 243).

Although Jesus taught messages of salvation and liberation through
other venues and used other examples, He used Peter's boat to illustrate
how to fish for people. While Jesus Himself in His human form was
not a fisherman by trade but a carpenter, He used fishing boats as a
means of transportation for ministry. Most often, the primary boats
that He used belong to one of His disciples like Peter, whose boat He
used first.

Prophetic Implications

The prophets had predicted the activities of Jesus in Peter's boat. Isaiah
wrote, "But there will be no more gloom for her who was in anguish
[for with judgment comes the promise of salvation]. In earlier times He
treated the land of Zebulun and the land of Naphtali with contempt,
but later on He will make them honored (by the presence of the
Messiah), by the way of the sea, on the other side of Jordan, Galilee of
the Gentiles" (Isiah 9:1 AB). White (1984) commented, "Looking down
through the ages, Jesus saw His faithful children in prison, in judgment
halls, in temptation, poverty, loneliness, and affliction. In the words
spoken to those gathered about Him on the shores of Gennesaret, He
was speaking also to these other souls the words that would come as a
message of hope in trial, comfort in sorrow, and light in darkness. That
voice speaking from the fisherman's boat would be heard speaking
peace to human hearts to the close of time."

The discourse ended. Jesus told Peter to launch out into the sea
and let down his net for a draught. However, Peter was disheartened
because all night he had caught nothing. During those lonely hours,

he had thought of John the Baptist languishing in his dungeon, of the prospect before Jesus and His followers, of the ill success of the mission to Judea, and of the malice of the priests and rabbis. As Peter watched by the empty nets, the future seemed dark with discouragement. "Master, we have toiled all the night, and have taken nothing: nevertheless, at Thy word I will let down the net" (Luke 5:5-11 KJV). After toiling all night without success, it seemed hopeless to cast the net into the clear waters of the lake, but love for their Master moved the disciples to obey. Simon and his brother let down the net. As they attempted to draw it in, so great was the quantity of fish that they were obliged to summon James and John to their aid. When the catch was secured, both Peter's boat and another one that belonged to another disciple were so heavily laden that they were in danger of sinking (White, 1984).

When we present ourselves to God as living vessels to be utilized for the salvation of others, God showers abundant blessings on us. The words of hope, peace, and blessings that Jesus spoke from Peter's boat were not only good news for Christians in that era but for followers of Christ until the second advent. At that time, Isaiah stated, "But there will be no more gloom for her who was in anguish." This appears to be a twofold prophecy for followers in Peter's time and Christians in the earth made new. "And God shall wipe all tears from their eyes; and there shall be no more death, neither sorrow, nor crying, neither shall there be any more pain: for the former things are passed away" (Revelation 21:4).

CHAPTER THREE

THE MAYFLOWER

We have witnessed divine occurrences operating throughout history to set the stage for the ushering in of God's eternal kingdom and the demolition of Satan's stronghold. He commissioned Noah to build an ark, which rendered a destructive blow to evil about two thousand four hundred and seventy years after creation. From about the first century BC, until AD 30, Peter's boat was one of the venues through which the kingdom of darkness received a death nail in its coffin that culminated at Golgotha. In the sixteenth century AD, Martin Luther delivered an unrecoverable jolt to the enemies of liberty of conscience by protesting papal and royal oppression. Years later, Luther's protest created a hunger in the soul in Christians in the old world of Rome to be free and set in motion the search for a liberty loving new world. Thus, through Providence, I believe, the *Mayflower* set sail.

PURPOSE AND ORIGIN OF THE *MAYFLOWER*

It is not clear how the *Mayflower* received its name, but we do know that it was named after a plant that bloomed in May. This plant was common in northern Europe, central Europe, and North America. Considering that the *Mayflower* plant bloomed and marked the month of May in both England and Massachusetts, it was an appropriate name for the ship. It was a symbol of home and renewed hope of freedom in a newfound land for the Pilgrims. They were reminded of their freedom each year when the *Mayflower* blossomed.

Johnson (2020) believed the builders of the *Mayflower* designed it to be a hundred feet long from stem to stern and twenty-four feet wide. In addition to its 102 passengers, the *Mayflower* carried a crew of thirty-seven sailors, cooks, carpenters, surgeons, and officers. On September 6, 1620, the boat set sail to America, loaded with weary Christians who were fleeing royal oppression and priestly intolerance with a determination to establish a government founded upon the broad foundation of freedom, civil, and religious liberty. This was exemplified after sixty-six days at sea when the ship landed safely at Cape Cod, November 9, 1620, one of the passengers, William Brewster led the Pilgrims to read Psalm 100 to give thanks to God for a successful crossing:

> Make a joyful noise unto the LORD, all ye lands. Serve
> the LORD with gladness: come before his presence with

singing. Know ye that the LORD he is God: it is he that hath made us, and not we ourselves; we are his people, and the sheep of his pasture. Enter into his gates with thanksgiving, and into his courts with praise: be thankful unto him and bless his name. (Psalm 100 KJV)

Among the Christian exiles who first fled to America and sought an asylum from royal persecution and priestly tyranny were many who determined to establish a government upon the broad foundation of civil and religious liberty. Their views were reflected in the Declaration of Independence, which sets forth the great truth that "all men are created equal" and endowed with the inalienable right to "life, liberty, and the pursuit of happiness." The Constitution guarantees to the people the right of self-government, providing that representative elected by the popular vote shall enact and administer the laws. Freedom of religious faith was also granted that every person is permitted to worship God according to the dictates of her conscience. Republicanism and Protestantism became the fundamental principles of the nation. These principles are the secret of its power and prosperity. The oppressed and downtrodden throughout Christendom have turned to this land with interest and hope. Millions have sought its shores, and through Providence, the United States has risen to a place among the most powerful nations of the earth.

White (1888) stated that freedom was so important to the pilgrims that in the grand old document that our founding fathers drafted as their bill of rights—the Declaration of Independence—they declared: "'We hold these truths to be self-evident, that all men are created equal; that they are endowed by their Creator with certain unalienable rights; that among these are life, liberty, and the pursuit of happiness.' The Constitution that they established guarantees, in the most explicit terms, the inviolability of conscience: 'No religious test shall ever be required as a qualification to any office of public trust under the United States.' 'Congress shall make no law respecting an establishment of religion or prohibiting the free exercise thereof.' The framers of the Constitution recognized the eternal principle that man's relation to his God is above human legislation, and his right of conscience inalienable. Reasoning was not necessary to establish this truth; we are conscious of it in our own bosom. It is this consciousness, which, in defiance of human laws, has sustained so many martyrs in tortures and flames. They believed that their duty to God was superior to human enactments, and that man could exercise no authority over their consciences. It is an inborn principle which nothing can eradicate."

White (1888) continues:

> As the tidings spread through the countries of Europe, of a land where every man might enjoy the fruit of his own labor, and obey the convictions of his conscience, thousands flocked to the shores of the New World. Colonies rapidly multiplied. "Massachusetts, by special law, offered free welcome and aid, at the public cost, to Christians of any nationality who might flee beyond the Atlantic 'to escape from wars or famine, or the oppression of their persecutors.' Thus the fugitive and the down-trodden were, by statute, made the guests of the commonwealth." In twenty years from the first landing at Plymouth, as many as a thousand Pilgrims were settled in New England (page 294).

The ancestors of one of the cofounders of the Adventist Church, Ellen G. White, were among the settlers who came directly from

England to New England in 1635 in search of the right to exercise freedom of conscience and to escape royal oppression. There is no direct evidence that they came on the *Mayflower* itself, but they did arrive on a boat (Joslyn 2002). The possible boats that they could have sailed on from England to America, that arrived in the ports of New England in 1635 may have been named as follows:

Christian;

Love;

Pied Cow;

Bachelor;

Rebecca; and

Mary Gould.

The above mentioned boats were possible vessels that Ellen's ancestors came to America on in search of freedom (Stevens 2022). To secure the objective which they pursued, they were content to earn a bare subsistence by a life of frugality and hard work. They expected nothing from the soil that they cultivated but the reasonable returns of their own sweat and labor. Like the apostle Paul, the settlers learned to be content with every situation that they found themselves in. They patiently endured the deprivations of the wilderness, watering the tree of liberty with their own tears and with the sweat of their brows until it took deep root in the newfound land.

Ellen White posited that the Bible was exalted as the foundation of their faith, the source of wisdom, and the charter of liberty and free choice. These principles were diligently and consistently taught in the home, in the school, and in the church, and the fruits were manifest in thrift, intelligence, purity, and temperance. If you could have lived among the settlers at that time, you would not have witnessed a drunkard, nor heard an imprecation, nor met a beggar. It was demonstrated that the principles of the Bible are the surest safeguards of national greatness. The feeble and isolated colonies grew to a confederation of powerful States, and the world marked with wonder the peace and prosperity of a church without a pope and a state without a king (White 1888).

Prophetic Implications

Bradford (2015) likened the *Mayflower* settlers to Ancient Israel, who also were pilgrims. "These all died in faith, not having received the promises, but having seen them afar off, and were persuaded of them, and embraced them, and confessed that they were strangers and pilgrims on the earth. For they that say such things declare plainly that they seek a country" (Hebrews 11:13, 14). Bradford posited:

> Our fathers were Englishmen who came over the great ocean and were ready to perish in the wilderness, but they cried to the Lord, and he heard their voice and looked on their adversity. When they wandered forth into the desert-wilderness, out of the way, and found no city to dwell in, both hungry and thirsty, their soul was overwhelmed in them.

Over a hundred years later, Benjamin Franklin, Thomas Jefferson, and John Adams proposed a seal for the new nation of the United States. It was an image of the ancient Israelites crossing the Red Sea with pharaoh chasing them and Moses standing on the other side, and would have included the motto "Rebellion to Tyrants is Obedience to God." Their obedience to God was their liberty, which is symbolized by the Liberty Bell that bears an inscription from Moses's book of Leviticus 25:10: "Proclaim liberty throughout all the Land unto all the Inhabitants thereof." Moses, the leader of the Israelites as they exited Egypt, is depicted on the eastern pediment of the United States Supreme Court building holding two tablets. He also appeared inside the courtroom, holding the Ten Commandments. Connections to Old Testament Israel are laced throughout America's political system, nods to the sojourners' tendency to identify with it. This fascination with an event nearly 3,500 years ago says a lot about America's religiopolitical identity and its future prophetic function (Frazier 2022).

Little did the settler realized that they were being directed by Providence to establish a nation that would initially have as its foundation liberty of conscience, but in the closing scenes of earth's history, the government will take away this liberty. John the prophet says, "I beheld another beast coming up out of the earth; and he had two horns like a lamb" (Revelation 13:11). Both the appearance of this beast and the manner of its rise indicate that the nation which it represents is unlike those presented under the preceding symbols in Revelation. The great kingdoms that have ruled the world were presented to the prophet Daniel as beasts of prey, rising when the "four winds of the heaven strove upon the great sea" (Daniel 7:2). In Revelation 17, an angel explained that waters represent "peoples, and multitudes, and nations, and tongues" (Revelation 17:15). Winds are a symbol of strife. The four winds of heaven striving upon the great sea represent the terrible scenes of conquest and revolution by which kingdoms previously have attained power.

However, the beast with lamblike horns was seen "coming up out of the earth." Instead of overthrowing other powers to establish itself, the nation thus represented must arise in territory previously unoccupied and unestablished as a nation and grow up gradually and peacefully. It could not, then, arise among the crowded and struggling nationalities of the Old World—that turbulent sea of "peoples, and multitudes, and nations, and tongues." It must be sought in the western continent. Although this land had some existing native inhabitants already, what nation of the New World was in 1798 rising into power? What nation was rapidly developing, giving promise of strength and greatness, and attracting the attention of the world? One nation, and only one, meets the specifications of this prophecy; it points unmistakably to the United States of America, which had its inception from the founders on the *Mayflower*.

White (1888) believed:

> Repeatedly, the thought, almost the exact words, of the sacred writer have been unconsciously employed by the orator and the historian in describing the rise and growth of this nation. The beast was seen "coming up out of the earth;" and, according to the translators, the word here rendered "coming up" literally signifies to "grow or spring up as a plant." And, as we have seen, the nation must arise in territory previously unoccupied and unestablished. A prominent writer, describing the rise of the United States, speaks of "the mystery of her coming forth from vacancy," and says, "Like a silent seed we grew into empire" (p. 462).

A European journal in 1850 spoke of the United States as a wonderful empire, which was "emerging" and "amid the silence of the earth daily adding to its power and pride" (*The Dublin Nation*). Edward Everett, in an oration on the Pilgrim founders of this nation, said, "Did they look for a retired spot, inoffensive from its obscurity, safe in its remoteness from the haunts of despots, where the little church of Leyden might enjoy freedom of conscience? Behold the mighty regions over which, in peaceful conquest, ... they have borne the banners of the cross." "And he had two horns like a lamb." The lamblike horns indicate youth, innocence, and gentleness, fitly representing the character of the United States when presented to the prophet as "coming up" in 1798 (Odom, 1958).

The Christian exiles who first fled to America sought an asylum from royal oppression and priestly intolerance, and they determined to establish a government upon the broad foundation of civil and religious liberty. Again, as previously mentioned in the chapter of the ark, I will repeat, the Declaration of Independence sets forth the great truth that "all men are created equal," and endowed with the inalienable right to "life, liberty, and the pursuit of happiness." And the Constitution guarantees to the people the right of self-government. Freedom of religious faith was also granted; every man being permitted to worship God according to the dictates of his conscience. Republicanism and Protestantism became the fundamental principles of the nation. These principles are the secret of its power and prosperity. The oppressed and downtrodden throughout Christendom have turned to this land with interest and hope. Millions have sought its shores of the United States.

The beast with lamblike horns "spake as a dragon. And he exercises all the power of the first beast before him, and causes the earth and them which dwell therein to worship the first beast, whose deadly wound was healed, ... saying to them that dwell on the earth, that they should make an image to the beast, which had the wound by a sword, and did live" (Revelation 13:11–14 NKJV).

The lamblike horns and dragon voice of the symbol point to a striking contradiction between the professions and the practice of the nation thus the "speaking" of the nation is the action of its legislative and judicial authorities. By such action, it will give the lie to those liberal and peaceful principles which it has put forth as the foundation of its policy. The prediction that it will speak "as a dragon," and exercise "all the power of the first beast," plainly foretells a development of the spirit of intolerance and persecution that was manifested by the nations represented by the dragon and the leopard-like beast. ("Apostate Protestantism Will Form the Image to the Beast"). And the statement that the beast with two horns "causes the earth and them which dwell therein to worship the first beast," indicates that the authority of this nation is to be exercised in enforcing Sunday observance which shall be an act of homage to the papacy.

Such action would be directly contrary to the freedom of religion principles of this government, to the genius of its free institutions, to the direct and solemn avowals of the Declaration of Independence, and to the Constitution. The founders of the nation wisely sought to guard against the employment of secular power on the part of the church, with its inevitable result—intolerance and persecution. The Constitution provides that "Congress shall make no law respecting an establishment of religion, or prohibiting the free exercise thereof," and that "no religious test shall ever be required as a qualification to any office of public trust under the United States." Only in flagrant violation of these safeguards to the nation's liberty, can any religious observance be enforced by civil authority. But the inconsistency of such action is no greater than is represented in the symbol. It is the beast with lamblike horns—in profession pure, gentle, and harmless— that speaks as a dragon. "Saying to them that dwell on the earth, that they should make an image to the beast." "The beast" whose worship is enforced is the first, or leopardlike, beast of Revelation 13—the papacy. The "image to the beast" represents that form of apostate Protestantism which will be developed when the Protestant churches seek the aid of civil power for the enforcement of their dogmas. This act is a violation of the Constitution because America is clearly a form of government in which the legislative power rests with the people; most striking evidence that the United States is the nation denoted in the prophecy (White1888).

Pilgrims on the *Mayflower* did not realize that they were a prophetic movement which predicted the rise and collapse of the Constitution of America. Prophecy describes a time when America will backslide from the Constitution and force "all people, great and small, rich and poor, free and bond, to receive a mark in their right hand, or in their foreheads" (Revelation 13: 13–16). White (1888) stated: "As the defenders of truth refuse to honor the Sunday-sabbath, some of them will be thrust into prison, some will be exiled, *some will be treated as slaves.* To human wisdom, all this now seems impossible; but as the restraining Spirit of God shall be withdrawn from men, and they shall be under the control of Satan, who hates the divine precepts, there will be strange developments. The heart can be very cruel when God's fear and love are removed" (p. 608).

CHAPTER FOUR

Ship Desire

The great thought of captains, owners, consignees, and others was to make the most money they could in the shortest possible time. Human nature is the same now as then.

—Fredrick Douglass

As stated in previous chapters, evil has persisted on earth since the Fall of the first human parents, Adam, and Eve. God admonished Noah to build an ark to stifle its infiltration and offer salvation to all as sin aggrandized. For the same liberating and salvific purposes

Jesus used Peter's vessel. As the hand of God continued to intervene in the course of history and execute his will, Protestants sought a new world via the use of the *Mayflower*. Paradoxically, in that same Century the first slave ship arrived in the newfound land of America. Slaves in the land of the free is a grand paradox that only God can help us understand. It was this implication of irony and hypocrisy that immediately arrested the attention of Christian abolitionists. To them, myopic and Capitalistic gain were primary factors that led slave traders to breach the Constitution. The group that participated in this constitutional violation was the crew that set sail on the ship *Desire*.

Purpose of Ship Desire

The purpose of the *Desire* is reflected in its name. Quant (2015) suggested that the naming of the first slave vessel *Desire* was symbolic of New England's desire to accumulate wealth as transporters of merchandise and slaves into various North American and Caribbean colonies. Operators maximized earnings by loading as many slaves as possible on the forty-nine tons, seventy-nine-foot *Desire*. They were able to cram seven hundred slaves onboard by chaining them together and grouping them in small spaces. This made their human cargo voyage more lucrative. However, the downside was that slaves on board were dehumanized, underfed, and brutally treated. This caused many to suffer poor health or die before reaching their destination. After which, the remains of these deceased slaves were dumped overboard as rubbish for the scavengers of the sea to consume.

Although brutal, the *Desire* carried out its design by making slave trading a very rewarding business in the Southern parts of America. The cheap labor of slaves enabled capitalists and slave masters to grow cotton and harvest billions of dollars in value over the years; especially after the cotton gin was invented. By the time of the Civil war, slaves had harvested enormous amount of cotton that it surpassed tobacco and was America's most popular crop. Cotton was called "white gold." Additionally, it was referred to as "King Cotton" because it was the major export of the United States in the early 1800s. By the 1850s, cotton grown, shipped, and sold by entrepreneurs in the south was worth more than all the rest of America's exports combined (*The American Civil War*).

Commerce was primarily sustained by slaves who were transported via the *Desire*. Although the *Desire* was not the first slave ship to arrive in America loaded with slaves, its impact on treating slaves as chattel to accumulates wealth was significant. A few years preceding the *Desire*, the ship *White Lion*, which was the first slave ship to arrive in Colonial America and docked in Jamestown, Virginia, August 1619, established the economical foundation for the *Desire* to build upon. However, the *Desire* not only imported slave to America, but it was also the first slave ship to export slaves from the United States (Philibert-Ortega 2014).

Ship *Desire*, which William Peirce was master, was the first boat to traffic enslaved people into Massachusetts Bay Colony. According to John Wintrop's journal, it was built in 1636 at Marblehead. It was built to serve multipurposed functions: To transport passengers, trade goods, and sale slaves. In July 1637, William Peirce, departed Massachusetts for Bermuda to sell into slavery fifteen Native Americans boys and two Native women who were captured in battle near New Haven. The following year in February Peirce returned on the *Desire* from Providence Island in the West Indies with a load of cotton, tobacco, and numerous of negros (Winthrop 1636).

Again, slave traders in general knew that many Africans would not survive the long, tedious, and dangerous trans-Atlantic journey through the middle passage. Therefore, they maximized the boat with slaves to compensate for the anticipated loss of lives in transit. Each slave occupied a tiny space of about ten to twelve inches and were chained and shackled together in pairs, which inhibited free movement, or at least made body rotation and repositioning difficult. The limited space and confined conditions precipitated the spread of smallpox, measles, dysentery, and many other diseases. Additionally, because of protracted duration of the trip, food and water was often in short supply and regularly rationed and many times completely ran out. Roughly a quarter of all those people transported out of Africa to the new world did not survive (British Library). This capturing of people led to massive loss of human lives, and human trafficking contradicted the United States' Constitution, which is the foundation of its government.

LAND OF THE FREE

Although the Ship *Desire* was strategically used to deliver people into bondage, God designed that they were transported to the "Land of the Free." God cannot interfere with humanity's free will because His love thrives on freedom of choice, even if it goes against God himself. He will not force us to do good. He stands at the door of our conscience and gently knocks, but He will never force entrance (Revelation 3:20). What God often does is interrupt the enemy's plans so that His will is ultimately triumphant. Joseph said to his brothers who sold him into slavery, "But as for you, you meant evil against me; but God meant it for good" (Genesis 5:20 NKJV). Regardless of the negative experiences in life, God is behind the scenes working all things out for our good and His purpose. James Russell Lawell wrote:

Truth forever on the scaffold, Wrong forever on the throne, yet that scaffold sways the future, and, behind the dim unknown, Standeth God within the shadow keeping watch above his own.

God did not interrupt the slave master's evil practice of slavery on the ship *Desire*, but He stood behind the scenes keeping watch over His own. This was illustrated by the fact that although slaves were inhumanly treated, build America through forced labor, but eventually gained their freedom because Providence had it that the Protestant framers of the Constitution guaranteed that all men are created equal. Slavery conflicted with the Constitution and created a paradoxical role of America. On the one hand, its Constitution promises the pursuit of freedom for all its inhabitants. Yet, on the other hand, Jim Crow was instituted to oppressed and enslave about 14 percent of its citizens. The very act of enslaving citizens contradicted democracy.

The oxymoronic idea of promising freedom to all but delivering slaves into bondage is represented by Lucifer from the very beginning in the garden of Eden, who overtly assured Adam and Eve freedom to become wise by knowing good and evil as God, while covertly enslaving them to sin. So, the concept of bondage had its origin on earth over six thousand years ago when Adam and Eve were deceived in Eden. The primary objective of the enemy is to promote the spirit of slavery to keep his subjects in captivity.

Contrarily, freedom is a fundamental and original design of God. The spirit of freedom is from God. Apostle Paul said, "Stand fast therefore in the liberty wherewith Christ hath made us free and be not entangled again with the yoke of bondage" (Galatians 5:1). "If the Son therefore shall make you free, ye shall be free indeed" (John 8:36 KJV). David said, "Restore unto me the joy of thy salvation; and uphold me with thy free spirit" (Psalm 51:12). God's free spirit has been in pursuit of sinners' restoration since the fall when Adam's offspring progressively plummeted into sin and God called Noah to construct an ark to deliver them.

The act of coercing human behavior originated in the kingdom of force, which belongs to Satan. The promotion of freedom of choice is from God's kingdom. Freedom and force are the two primary opposing entities in the battle between good and evil. This is illustrated in the Bible when the disciples competed among themselves for positions of power and debated about which one of them would be the greatest in the kingdom of heaven (Matthew 18:4). To contextualize the argument, White (2002) stated:

> The Savior gathered His disciples about Him, and said to them, "If any man desire to be first, the same shall be last of all, and servant of all." There was in these words a solemnity and impressiveness which the disciples were far from comprehending. That which Christ discerned they could not see. They did not understand the nature of Christ's kingdom, and this ignorance was the apparent cause of their contention. But the real cause lay deeper. By explaining the nature of the kingdom, Christ might for the time have quelled their strife; but this would not have touched the underlying cause. Even after they had received the fullest knowledge, any question of precedence might have renewed the trouble. Thus, disaster would have been brought to the church after Christ's departure. The strife for the highest place was the outworking of that same spirit which was the beginning of the great controversy in

the worlds above, and which had brought Christ from heaven to die. There rose up before Him a vision of Lucifer, the "son of the morning," in glory surpassing all the angels that surround the throne, and united in closest ties to the Son of God. Lucifer had said, "I will be like the Most High" (Isaiah 14:12, 14); and the desire for self-exaltation had brought strife into the heavenly courts, and had banished a multitude of the hosts of God. Had Lucifer really desired to be like the Most High, he would never have deserted his appointed place in heaven; for the spirit of the Most High is manifested in unselfish ministry. Lucifer desired God's power, but not His character. He sought for himself the highest place, and every being who is actuated by his spirit will do the same. Thus alienation, discord, and strife will be inevitable. Dominion becomes the prize of the strongest. The kingdom of Satan is a kingdom of force; every individual regards every other as an obstacle in the way of his own advancement, or a steppingstone on which he himself may climb to a higher place (p. 435).

Masters of the *Desire*, motivated by myopic interest, is a depiction of the kingdom of force that insistently enslaved people, a course of action in direct opposition to the kingdom of freedom that Jesus offers. Crewmembers of the boat unfortunately changed the social behavior of free Africans by kidnapping them from their native land and transporting them to America in chains. The process of making and socializing Africans to be slaves was immediately initiated upon boarding the slave ship. The use of shackles, chains, and handcuffs were not only used to prevent the slaves from escaping but to dominate and humiliate them. This barbaric treatment was an example of how they would be treated by their masters on the plantation. Slave masters physically and psychologically controlled their slaves as prison guards did to prisoners, which suggested to the slaves, who committed no crime, that they were criminals and deserving of such punishment (Peace Ezebuiro 2020). This codependent and abusive relationship would be perpetuated for generations and become the norm for future interaction of offspring of slaves and their slave masters.

Even unlearned slaves never accepted their physical bondage because they understood that freedom is God's gift to His creation. God has placed in the spirit of each person and each creature a will to be free. A wild animal will often-time chew off portions of its leg to escape from the trap. An untamed caged bird will sometimes flap its wings against the crate until they become bloody to go free. As other members of God's creation, human beings will sacrifice their lives to be free. The civil rights freedom fighters sang, "Before I be a slave I'll be buried in my grave and go home to my Lord and be free." Apostle Paul says to humans who are created in the image of God, "Stand fast therefore in the liberty wherewith Christ hath made us free and be not entangled again with the yoke of bondage" (Galatians 5:1 KJV). Paul is comparing the liberty of the gospel to the bondage of the ceremonial system, through which the Judaizers wanted to force the new converts in Galatia to be circumcised. The truth of Jesus creates a longing in our hearts for freedom in its a totality; spiritually, physically, and psychologically.

The inconsistent nature of the "Land of the Free," America, is that its Constitution guarantees freedom and liberty for all, yet it kidnapped Africans from their homeland, oppressed, and forced them into slave labor. America speaks as a lamb through the Christian principles in its Constitution but behaves like a dragon when it violates human rights and dehumanizes, lynches, and tyrannizes people whose rights are guaranteed. This constitutional breach was irreligious in principle and was precipitated by capitalistic greed. Interestingly, they desired freedom from priestly and royal oppression for themselves, which is why they fled the Old World, but had no problem oppressing others in the New World.

Spiritual Symbolism

The *Desire* slave boat was symbolic of physical captivity and is reflective of the spiritual bondage of the enslavers. Slave masters projected their own brokenness on their slaves, which is paralleled to what Satan does when he captures humans in his grip. He takes delight in keeping humanity on his plantation of vice fettered and shackled in the bondage of evil and of sin as he himself is. White (1882) specified:

> I was shown Satan as he once was, a happy, exalted angel. Then I was shown him as he now is. He still bears a kingly form. His features are still noble, for he is an angel fallen. But the expression of his countenance is full of anxiety, care, unhappiness, malice, hate, mischief, deceit, and every evil. That brow, which was once so noble, I particularly noticed. His forehead commenced from his eyes to recede. I saw that he had so long bent himself to evil that every good quality was debased, and every evil trait was developed. His eyes were cunning, sly, and showed great penetration. His frame was large, but the flesh hung loosely about his hands and face. As I beheld him, his chin was resting upon his left hand. He appeared to be in deep thought.

A smile was upon his countenance, which made me tremble, it was so full of evil and satanic slyness. This smile is the one he wears just before he makes sure of his victim, and as he fastens the victim in his snare, this smile grows horrible (p. 151).

The enemy is broken, immersed in sin, and this condition he seeks to project and displace on humans. He wants the inhabitants of earth to suffer eternal damnation with him. His joy comes from enslaving humans in iniquity. Ellen White says he smiles when he is sure of his victim, and this made her tremble. However, there is no need to fear because Jesus has paid the price and redeemed us from the bondage of immorality. Calvary was our Emancipation Proclamation written in the blood of Jesus.

SCIENTIFIC AND PSYCHOLOGICAL BONDAGE

Part of the process of making slaves is to break their will. This process was initiated by chaining their arms and legs before loading them on the ship *Desire*. Additionally, slave traders used brutal beatings fear tactics to break their will. After the slaves go through the breaking process and still attempted to escape, they were considered by their slave master to have a psychological disorder, instead of understanding that their desire to be free is an innate response that God gave them.

During the early years of slavery psychologists and psychiatrists did not understand the slaves' unrelenting desire to be free despite draconian punishment. This is reflected is their response to a slave's repeated attempts to escape regardless of the threat of lynching. Samuel Cartwright, a doctor at that time, diagnosed the bond servant's desire to be free, "drapetomania," a psychological disorder. Cartwright stated that this disorder was caused by the slave master becoming too familiar with their slaves and treating them as equals. His prescribed treatment for this disease was to severely beat the slave. Plantation overseers were encouraged to utilize whipping as the primary intervention once the disease had progressed to the stage of actually running away. In essence, Cartwright suggested that Negros should be kept in a submissive state and treated as children ... to prevent and cure them from running away (Jackson 2015).

Benjamin Rush (1746–1813), a signer of the Declaration of Independence, dean of the medical school at the University of Pennsylvania, and father of American psychiatry, described Negroes as people who suffered from an affliction called "Negritude." He thought this disorder was a mild form of leprosy that could sometimes cause discoloration of their skin. As leprosy, he said, Blacks needed to be quarantined from others to prevent spreading the infections. Additionally, Blacks should not intermarry because their children would be infected. Rush suggested that Africans became insane soon after they were put in slavery in the West Indies. He stated that the traumatic impact of slavery and oppression had a perpetual effect on slaves and their descendants (Jackson 2015). These traumas were revealed years later by the American Psychiatric Association.

One hundred and seventy-five years after its finding, the American Psychiatric Association apologized for professional psychiatrists practice of scientific racism. To name a few, consider the following:

- Benjamin Rush, America's first psychiatrist, who used a method for taming horses in Great Britain to tame slaves. He would confine them in a solitary dark room and force them to stand upright in increments of three days, while pricking them with pointed nails to prevent sleeping. This treatment he thought would subdue and make slaves more docile.

- In 1951 Walter Freeman performed lobotomies on Black patients at the Veterans Administration hospital in Tuskegee, Alabama. He described the procedures as surgically induced childhood, in which he cut into the brain to alter its original structure to create a submissive behavior.

- Psychologist Francis Galton in 1883 created a term called *eugenics*, meaning "good stock." It is based on the idea that some cultural groups are inferior to others. He considered Africans to be inferior to Whites. He stated, "These savages (ask for) slavery." This is his justification for brutally responding to slaves' desire to be free.

- In 1960 psychiatrists invented a disorder named "protest psychosis" to stereotype African Americans who participated in the civil rights movement as aggressive. All who marched and protested were said to be schizophrenic. Antipsychotic drugs were advertised and prescribed to Blacks. Even today, African Americans are disproportionately prescribed antipsychotic drugs (Citizens Commission on Human Rights of Colorado 2021).

The longing to be free is not a psychological disorder but a divine design. When God created celestials and humans, He demonstrated His love by granting them the gift of free will; the ability to exercise freedom of conscience and of choice. This ability to choose your own destiny originated with the Creator. Jesus said of His mission," The Spirit of the Lord is upon me, because He has anointed Me to preach good news to the poor. He has sent me to proclaim liberty to the captives" (Luke 4:18 NIV). God hardwired a hunger for liberty in the DNA of all created beings. It was more desired among slaves than life itself. Again, they sang, "Before I be a slave I'll be buried in my grave and go home to my Lord and be free."

Freedom was on the minds of the millions of slaves who were transported not only by the ship *Desire*, but by all British slave ships from the years 1700 up to 1808. Their hopes and dreams begun to materialize when, according to the "Slave Trade Act of 1807 by United Kingdom of Great Britain and Ireland Act of Parliament 47 Geo. 3 session 1c. 36," the slave trade was abolished. Although slavery illegally continued for about another fifty years, the government of the United States officially abolished slave trading in 1808. However, it was not until 1863 when Abraham Lincoln signed the Emancipation Proclamation, that physical slavery was terminated. Nevertheless, the propensities to enslave yet exist today because the oppressors harbor the spirit of slavery in their hearts.

Soteriological Metaphors

Passengers on each of the crafts in this book, and boats in general, had various experiences that led many in contemporary society to apply the risks, danger, and shelter of voyages metaphorically by making salvific applications to their own lives. We often hear people use phrases like the following:

- "We all are on the same boat."
- "With holes in your boat, you cannot go anywhere."
- "Get in the ark of safety."
- "Don't rock the boat."

African slaves who were brought to America via boats faced many adversities in route, which continued after their arrival. As a result, the United Nations estimated the over 17 million slaves perished from suicide, homicide, and diseases (World Future Fund 2001). The number of slaves that perished can be compared to the individual populations of Syria, Cambodia, Senegal, Chad, Somalia, Zimbabwe, Ecuador, and Guatemala. However, despite the danger of the water, deaths of acquaintances and friends that they witnessed in transit to America, slaves reimagined the usage of boats and transform them from vessels of horror into metaphors of salvation and liberation. Their longing to be free manifested itself in metaphorical songs that were reflected in the lyrics of the "Old Ship of Zion":

> I was drifting away on life's pitiless sea,
> And the angry waves threatened my ruin to be,
> When away at my side, there I dimly descried,
> A stately old vessel, and loudly I cried:
> Ship ahoy! Ship ahoy!
> And loudly I cried: Ship ahoy!
>
> 'Twas the old ship of Zion, thus sailing along,
> All aboard her seemed joyous,
> I heard their sweet song;
> And the captain's kind ear, ever ready to hear,
> Caught my wail of distress, as I cried out in fear:
> Ship ahoy! Ship ahoy!
> As I cried out in fear: Ship ahoy!
>
> The good captain commanded a boat to be low'red,
> And with tender compassion He took me on board;
> And I'm happy today, all my sins washed away
> In the blood of my Savior, and now I can say:
> Bless the Lord! Bless the Lord!
> From my soul I can say: Bless the Lord!

O soul, sinking down 'neath sin's merciless wave,

The strong arm of our captain is mighty to save;

Then trust Him today, no longer delay,

Board the old ship of Zion, and shout on your way:

Jesus saves! Jesus saves!

Shout and sing on your way: Jesus saves!

(M. J. Cartwright 1889).

Another spiritual that reflected the slaves' perspective of boats as symbols of salvation and liberation is the spiritual "Michael, Row Your Boat Ashore." Michael in the song is the Archangel—Jesus. The shore references the Jordan River, which is symbolic for the gulf that divides earth and heaven, and the boat is a vessel of liberation. The lyrics are as follows:

Michael, row the boat a-shore

Hallelujah!

Then you'll hear the trumpet blow

Hallelujah!

Then you'll hear the trumpet sound,

Hallelujah!

Trumpet sound the world around

Hallelujah!

Trumpet sound the jubilee

Hallelujah!

Trumpet sound for you and me

Hallelujah! (Allen, Ware, and Garrison 1867).

"Michael, Row Your Boat Ashore" is a spiritual that was first sung by former slaves. It was initially heard during the American Civil War at St. Helena Island, which was one of the Sea Islands of South Carolina.

This song was rendered by African Americans whose owners had abandoned the island before the union Navy would come, disembark, and enforce a blockade. Charles Picard Ware, an abolitionist and Harvard graduate who had come to supervise the plantation on St. Helena from 1862 to 1865, transcribed the song in musical notation as he heard former slaves sing it. Ware's cousin, William Francis Allen reported that while he rode in a boat across Station Creek, the former slaves sang the song as they rowed (Epstin 2003).

Prophetic Implications

As horrendous as the Ship *Desire* transatlantic voyage was, it had prophetic implications. White (2005) stated that slavery will be revived in the South. Interestingly, according to Revelation 6:15, 16, there will be slavery at the second advent of Christ. Here we find the phrase "every bondman, and every free man" will be forced into slavery. The statement by Ellen White indicates that she was shown in vision slaves and slave masters will exist at the second advent of Christ. In this she is in perfect accord with the Bible. Both John the prophet and Mrs. White were shown conditions that would exist at the second coming of our Lord. In 1895, three decades after the Emancipation Proclamation was signed, Ellen White provided even greater clarity and was more specific on the topic. She iterated: "At present, Sunday keeping is not the test. The time will come when men will not only forbid Sunday work, but they will try to force men to labor on the Sabbath. And men will be asked to renounce the Sabbath and to subscribe to Sunday observance or forfeit their freedom and their lives. But the time for this has not yet come, for the truth must be presented more fully before the people as a witness … Slavery will again be revived in the Southern States; for the spirit of slavery still lives (p. 276).

Slave traders on the ship *Desire* promoted the spirit of slavery by contributing to the establishment of the slave system in America. The spirit of slavery is instigated and influenced by Satan. This spirit was manifested in the oppressive system of Jim Crow; segregation, disenfranchisement, dehumanization, lynching, and all the laws that that made it illegal for Blacks to receive an education, equal treatment under the law, and freedom from oppression. The way Ellen G. White (1889) explained it to those who were ministering to Blacks in the South is as follows:

> My children, you will meet with deplorable ignorance. Why? Because the souls that were kept in bondage were taught to do exactly the will of those who called them their property and held them as slaves. They were kept in ignorance and were untaught. Thousands of them do not know how to read. Their teachers are, many of them, corrupt in character, and they read the Scriptures to fulfill their own purposes, to degrade in life and practice. They are taught that they must not think or judge for themselves, but their ministers must judge for them. In their teaching the divine plan has been covered up by a mass of rubbish and falsehood and perversion of the Scriptures ... This is a favorable field for the working of seducing spirits, and they will have success, because of the ignorance of the human minds so long trammeled and abused as their bodies have been. The whole system of slavery (Jim Crow) was originated by Satan, the tyrant over human beings whenever the opportunity offers for him to oppress. Whenever he can get the chance, he ruins (p. 5.1).

White also explains,

> For the spirit of slavery still lives … Many have the spirit
> of the devil working in them still. In every way possible
> they will oppose everything that has a tendency to lift
> up the colored race (p.299).

Brown (2020) further explained the elements of the spirit of slavery
when he stated:

> From 1877 to 1950, more than 4,400 black men,
> women, and children were lynched by white mobs,
> according to the Equal Justice Initiative. Black people
> were shot, skinned, burned alive, bludgeoned, and
> hanged from trees. Lynchings were often conducted
> within sight of the institutions of justice, on the lawns
> of courthouses. Some historians say the violence
> against thousands of black people who were lynched
> after the Civil War is the precursor to the vigilante
> attacks and abusive police tactics still used against
> black people today, usually with impunity. To name
> a few: George Floyd's death May 25, 2020, came six
> weeks after police in Louisville, Kentucky, March 13,
> 2020, fatally shot Breonna Taylor, a 26-year-old black
> woman, during a midnight "no-knock" raid on her
> home. It came 10 weeks, February 23, 2020, after the
> killing of Ahmaud Arbery, a 25-year-old black man,
> who was chased down by a white father and son in
> a pickup truck as he jogged in his neighborhood in
> Glynn County, Georgia.

According to Adventist pioneers and Bible prophecy, America and the spirit of slavery are both prophetic. This great country of ours that has for its foundation the Constitution which declares that all men are created equal will one day turn its back on its own laws and again enslave its citizens near the end of time. Scripture informs us that the republican form of government that we currently enjoy will be denounced for totalitarianism, autocracy, communism, or a religiopolitical authoritarian type of government that promotes one religion as truth and persecute none-conformers. At this time slavery on a broader scale will be reinstituted in a manner that humanity has never witness. "He causes all, both small and great, rich and poor, free and slaves, to receive a mark on their right hand or on their forehead, and that no man may buy or sell except one who has the mark or the name of the beast, or the number of his name" (Revelation 13:16, 17).

CHAPTER FIVE

THE MORNING STAR

The *Morning Star* is the concluding of the legendary vessels to be discussed. Its primary purpose was compatible to the mission of Noah's ark, Peter's fishing boat, and the *Mayflower*, which was liberation from the oppressiveness of evil forces. Contrarily, the *Desire* slave ship contributed to the establishment and the perpetuation of systemic slavery. Additionally, the *Desire* gave rise to Jim Crow, which prohibited Blacks from receiving an education by making it illegal for a slave to read, thereby intentionally prolonged their bondage. However, the *Morning Star* was built in response to the system of slavery and its barbaric practices by endeavoring to liberate slaves. Edson White, the builder of the *Morning Star* advocated that education, which contains the truth of God's Word, is a source of restoration and liberation of conscience. Freedom is realized when the mind is unfettered and fused with God's Word.

MOTIVATION AND DESIGN OF THE *MORNING STAR*

As the ship *Desire* and other slave vessels were designed to enslave people, the *Morning Star* was designed to set the captives free. This endeavor ensued following the Adventists' antislavery stance, in 1894 at the age of forty-five, Edson White started a boatbuilding project in Allegan, Michigan. His goal was to build a paddlewheel steamer that could be used as a portable church and school to educate former slaves and their children. He designed the boat to be twelve feet wide and seventy-two feet long. It was engineered to have a chapel, print shop, darkroom, library, kitchen, storage areas, and an apartment for the crew (Graybill 1971). The *Morning Star* brought bright hope to the downtrodden people of color.

This missionary vessel was named *Morning Star* because of its biblical connotation. As the Bible states, Jesus called himself, "the bright and *morning star*" (Revelation 22:16). The Apostle Peter iterated, "And so we have the prophetic word confirmed, which you do well to heed as a light that shines in a dark place, until the day dawns and the morning star rises in your heart (2 Peter 1:19). The *Morning Star*, also known as the missionary steamer, was built to deliver the prophetic light from the books of Daniel and Revelation and the gospel of Jesus Christ to areas of the South that had been darkened by the sin of slavery. The light that this boat bore delivered enlightened messages of freedom and hope to African Americans who resided primarily in the Southern domains of America.

After Ellen White's appeal to her son and recounted an epiphany of his perils shown to her as one endangered by the undertow, Edson White experienced a thorough reconversion and desired again to enter the service of the Lord. Ellen White fully understood the forthcoming attacks of the enemy as he attempts to regain his lost prey. Therefore, she wrote Edson often to encourage and caution him. Aware of the danger of embarking upon such monumental task, he nonetheless pursued it passionately because his heart had been stirred as he read while in Battle Creek his mother's appeal for something to be done among the neglected blacks in the Southern States.

He wrote exuberant letters to his mother detailing his plans to build a missionary boat and sail down the Mississippi River and use it as a base for work among the blacks. Knowing Edson's proclivity for adventure and his weakness in handling business matters, Ellen White entertained misunderstanding regarding his motive. She thought that perhaps he had reverted to his preconversion manner of thinking. For this reason, she wished he and his wife, Emma, could be with her in Australia. She wrote regarding the boat on May 2, "I can only say, the will of the Lord be done." If this is the Lord's plan, I have not a sign of an objection to it; but I feel deeply over the fact that you are not with us in the work. I am more disappointed than I can express. ... I have not been able to get over this disappointment without tears (Letter 79, 1894).

The *Morning Star* was built on the banks of the Kalamazoo River at Allegan, Michigan, in 1894, after Edson's reconversion. It was his ambition, and the ambition of his close friend Will Palmer, to initiate missional work among the blacks in the Deep South. The boat was designed with a threefold purpose, which are as follows:

- transportation along the twisting waterways of the Mississippi and its tributaries
- a house for the workers
- a portable meeting place for the people

As the boat neared completion, it sailed under its own steam down the river to Douglass, a port on the east side of Lake Michigan. There Edson hired a fruit steamer, the *Bon Ami*, to tow the *Morning Star* with its own engines running, across the lake to Chicago. It was a night's journey. On their way a violent storm arose. The steam tubes of the *Morning Star* clogged and the hull began to fill with water, nearly sinking the craft. Fourteen hours after leaving the Michigan port, the exhausted crews of the two boats stepped ashore in Chicago. The captain of the *Bon Ami* gave Edson a ten-dollar donation, saying it was something more than human power that had brought them through the storm (Graybill 1971).

From Chicago, the *Morning Star*, with Emma, Edson's wife, on board, and with an enlarging crew, passed through the Illinois and Michigan Canal to LaSalle, Illinois, down the Illinois River to the Mississippi, and on down to Vicksburg, where it landed on January 10, 1895. Along the route Edson had picked up a team of workers, including Fred Halladay, who would spend the next fifteen years in service to the blacks of the American South.

Although the boat was built originally with one deck, the steamer was lengthened and widened in 1897, and received an extra deck. This increased the capacity for greater quality of work. When Ellen White first saw the *Morning Star* it had been redesigned. It was now rendered appropriate for occasional usage in meetings while it was at Centennial Lake in Vicksburg, but the work had to be established ashore before the steamer could do her best service along the Yazoo River (Graybill 1971).

White (1901) recapitulated:

> While in Vicksburg I made my home on "The *Morning*
> *Star*," and I looked to see the great extravagance
> which I had heard had been manifested by my son
> Edson in the preparation of this boat as a house to
> live in, as a meetinghouse to which he could call the
> people to hear the truth as he went up and down
> the river. What did I see? I saw the plainest little
> rooms, some merely lined with plain boards. There
> was not one extravagant thing in the boat. Now to
> those who are troubled about the wrongs done in
> these missionary fields, I would say, why don't you
> have interest enough to go there, and see what is
> being done, before you nourish your prejudices? Why
> do you not interest yourself enough in the field to
> become acquainted with it to prove all things? Then
> you will testify that the work being done is right and
> good (General Conference Bulletin 1901).

Edson begun his Vicksburg work with Sunday schools and night classes in the Mount Zion Baptist church on Fort Hill. When he was excluded from the church for his belief in the Sabbath, he built a little chapel at the corner of Walnut and First East streets. But this was only after ten days of fervent prayer had resulted in permission from adamant city councilmen to grant a permit for building a church for the blacks. However, the little chapel and schoolhouse outgrew its capacity, and Ellen White was on hand to dedicate the new and enlarged church during her 1901 visit. The present Vicksburg church stands on the site of this second building, and in the early 1970s three women who had been aboard the *Morning Star* were still worshiping there.

Edson apparently had explained to his mother that after the work was established in Vicksburg, they ventured into the heart of the delta, using the Yazoo River as their main highway. Halfway up the river to Yazoo City, he had tried to establish a school for the hundreds of black children in the area who had no facilities for education. He was soon informed by the county superintendent of education that his work must stop, and later learned that in the mob that accompanied the superintendent was one man who had volunteered to hold a Winchester rifle on Edson while a rope was gathered to retain him.

Later, the work there was stopped. On the boat Edson had edited and published a monthly journal, the *Gospel Herald*. One issue carried a mildly critical editorial of the sharecropper system, and this, along with the fact that so many of the blacks were becoming Adventists and refusing to work on Saturdays, spurred the plantation owners to action. A mob of twenty-five White men on horseback called at the school, sent the white teacher, one of Edson's men, out of town "on a rail," nailed the doors and windows shut, and burned books, maps, and charts in the schoolyard. Then they found one of the leading black believers in the area, N. W. Olvin, and thrashed him with a buggy whip, stopping only when commanded to do so by a white man who brandished a revolver (Graybill 1971).

One hair-raising episode that Edson encountered was the time the *Morning Star* escaped being dynamited in Yazoo City, having left town only hours earlier with the General Conference president and secretary on board. F. R. Rogers, who taught the Yazoo City school, was ordered by a mob to close his school, and was shot at in the streets. Additionally, these early workers and believers faced two kinds of prejudices, racial and religious. The black ministers opposed them because they were teaching Sabbath observance and tithe paying; the white people opposed them because they were educating the blacks and introducing new and better agricultural methods, which threatened to break the stranglehold of poverty in the Delta.

Edson had informed his mother of these developments during her years in Australia, and her instruction was of caution and prudence as the only course available to the church if they wished to continue to witness and work in the South. This was as true for the work among the whites as among the blacks. Even though in his contacts Edson said nothing about political matters, even though he did not mention inequalities or the need for social justice, the mere fact that he was educating blacks and trying to improve their economic condition nearly cost him his life and the lives of his wife, fellow workers, and believers (Graybill 1971).

PROPHETIC IMPLICATIONS

Years before Edson White built the *Morning Star*, due to its prophetic inferences, Adventist pioneers opposed slavery. In reference to the two-horned beast, the first Adventist to connect American slavery with the lamblike beast "speaking like a dragon" in Revelation 13 was the young Adventist scholar John Nevins Andrews. According to Andrews, who would go on to become the church's first official missionary and its third General Conference president, slavery was a wicked and evil practice, and it was one of the attributes of the two-horned beast. In the article of the *Advent Review* entitled "Thoughts on Revelation 13 and 14," Andrews (1851) suggested:

> Civil and religious power, differing in many respects
> from those, which have preceded it. It is in appearance

the mildest form of power which ever existed, but it is after having deceived the world with its wonders, to exhibit all the tyranny of the first beast. Are the pretensions of this power well founded? Let us examine. If all men are born free and equal, how do we then hold three million of slaves in bondage? Why is it that the Negro race are reduced to the rank of chattels personnel, and bought and sold like brute beasts? If the right of private judgment be allowed, why then are men expelled from these religious bodies for no greater crime than that of attempting to obey God in something where in the word of God may not be in accordance with their creed? (p. 84).

Hiram Edson, another Adventist pioneer, pointed out that the Lamb-like Beast from Revelation 13:11–18 represents American Protestantism. Edson position was that soon America would join ranks with the Papacy to form a new world superpower. He explained that the Catholic Church received a "mortal wound" (Revelation 13:1–10) and lost its authority over the secular nations through the events of the French Revolution. Nevertheless, America will, in the near future, "heal the wounded head" of the papal beast (Revelation 13:12) and reunite the church and state, persecuting the religious dissenters once more (Edson 1850, p. 9). The major Adventist leaders of the time including James White, Joseph Bates, and Otis Nichols all agreed with Hiram Edson's interpretation.

Uriah Smith (1853) is another Adventist pioneer, who spoke vehemently against America's practice of slavery in a poem that was published in the Advent Review and Sabbath Herald:

With two horns like a lamb a beast arose-
So, with two leading forms a power has risen,
two fundamental principles, than which
In all the earth none can be found more mild,
More lamb-like in their outward form and name.
A land of freedom, pillared on the broad
And open basis of equality;
A land reposing 'neath the gentle sway
of civil and religious liberty.
Lamb-like in form, is there no dragon-voice
Heard in our land? No notes that harshly grate
Upon the ear of mercy, love and truth?
And put humanity to open shame?
Let the united cry of millions tell-
Millions that groan beneath oppression's rod,
Beneath the sin-forged chains of slavery,
Robbed of their rights, to brutes degraded down,
And soul and body bound to other's will
Let their united cries, and tears, and groans,
That daily rise, and call aloud on Heaven
For vengeance, answer; let the slave reply.
O land of boasted freedom! Thou hast given
The lie to all thy loud professions, first,
of justice, liberty and equal rights;
And thou hast set a foul and heinous blot
upon the sacred page of liberty;
And whilst thou traffickest in souls of men,
Thou hurl'st defiance, proud, in face of Heaven
Soon to be answered with avenging doom. (p. 8)

This poem is Uriah Smith's presentation of America as the lamblike beast in the book of Revelation is revealed in a sequence of statements and articles that he published comparing America's lamblike profession with its dragonlike behavior. Additionally, Loughborough's (1858) characterization of America as a lamblike beast is as follows:

> This is all revealed to us in one sentence, short indeed, but abundant in meaning: Revelation 13:11) "And he had two horns like a lamb, and he spake as a dragon." Out of the abundance of the heart the mouth speaketh; therefore the animal has a dragon's heart. His disposition, his motives, intentions, desires, are all like a dragon; his outward appearance, his horns, which must of course be prominent objects to the beholder, his open profession, are all lamb-like. His appearance is good enough, and we might be led to look upon him as a whole, as quite an amiable creature, were it not that when he raises his voice in acts of authority, he speaks as a dragon: like the old fable of the ass in the lion's skin; if he only had not brayed, his fellow-beasts would have taken him for a lion (p. 167–168).

James White, Ellen's husband was also antislavery. To expose the hypocrisy of America, White (1861) wrote:

> Many things are esteemed sacred in America; the most sacred thing is slavery. The Constitution is held sacred, but not so sacred as slavery. When the two come in contact it is the Constitution that has to give way. When the Constitution is found to be against slavery it is the Constitution that is to be "amended." ... Liberty

is held sacred, but not so sacred as slavery. Where slavery appears, liberty hides her head and vanishes, of course ... The Bible is held sacred, but not so sacred as slavery. Its Decalogue, its golden rule, its law, its gospel, are all revised and set aside by the code of slavery. It annuls marriage, with-holds the Bible, enforces labor without wages, and sells the temple of the Holy Ghost as a chattel, and remains a Bible institution still! ... Nationality is held sacred, but not so sacred as slavery. When slavery calls for secession, nationality is cast off as an abhorred thing (p. 17).

James White published this article two months after the attack at Fort Sumter, which was after the South seceded and during the naval blockade. At this time, Lincoln had not issued a call for troops, and the Civil war had not intensified. James highlighted that slavery was so sacred to the Southerner that they would rather engage in a bloody civil war than relinquish it.

Long before Edson built the *Morning Star*, he understood from his parents the history and mentality of slave owners in the South and the challenges that he would encounter in his venture to meet his objective. He also was aware of the value of using a boat that was retrofitted for multiple purposes. He would use it to liberate the souls of "Colored People" (African Americans) from the effects of the oppression of slavery and of "Jim Crow." The methods that he used were holistic: mental, physical, and spiritual. He established educational institutions to improve the slaves' mental outlook, which also improved their physical and spiritual wellbeing. "When the mind of man is brought into communion with the mind of God, the finite with the Infinite, the effect on body and mind and soul is beyond estimate. In such communion is found the highest education. It is God's own method of development. "Acquaint now thyself with Him" (Job 22:21) is His message to mankind (White 1911, p. 125).

The health message and dietary laws are a vital part of the gospel and was especially needed to uplift former slaves, whose diet consisted of health debilitating scrap flesh meat of animals such as pig feet, tail, chitterlings, and ears. The message of health restored vitality and prolonged life. "When properly conducted, the health work is an entering wedge, making a way for other truths to reach the heart. When the third angel's message is received in its fullness, health reform will be given its place in the councils of the conference, in the work of the church, in the home, at the table, and in all the household arrangements. Then the right arm will serve and protect the body and to nurture their physical being, and the gospel served to set them free from the bondage of sin" (White 1953, p. 72).

The third angel's message is in Revelation 14:6–10 and it is followed by the first and second angel messages:

> And I saw another angel fly in the midst of heaven, having the everlasting gospel to preach unto them that dwell on the earth, and to every nation, and kindred, and tongue, and people, Saying with a loud voice, Fear God, and give glory to him; for the hour of his judgment is come: and worship him that made heaven, and earth, and the sea, and the fountains of waters. And there followed another angel, saying, Babylon is fallen, is fallen, that great city, because she made all nations drink of the wine of the wrath of her fornication. And the third angel followed them, saying with a loud voice, If any man worship the beast

and his image, and receive his mark in his forehead, or in his hand, The same shall drink of the wine of the wrath of God, which is poured out without mixture into the cup of his indignation; and he shall be tormented with fire and brimstone in the presence of the holy angels, and in the presence of the Lamb (Rev. 14:6–10).

In prophecy, this warning against receiving the mark of the beast and avoiding the negative consequences of God's judgment with its connected messages is followed by the coming of the Son of Man in the clouds of heaven. The proclamation of the judgment is an announcement that Christ's second coming is at hand. And this proclamation is called the everlasting gospel. Thus, the preaching of Christ's second coming, the announcement of its nearness, is shown to have been an essential part of the gospel message that Edson delivered from the *Morning Star*. Slavery was emblematic of a Luciferian spirit that is characterized by secularism. The Bible declares that in the last days men will be absorbed in worldly pursuits, in pleasure and the accumulation of wealth. They will be blind to eternal realities. Christ says, "As the days of Noah were, so shall also the coming of the Son of man be. For as in the days that were before the flood they were eating and drinking, marrying and giving in marriage, until the day that Noah entered into the ark, and knew not until the flood came, and took them all away; so shall also the coming of the Son of man be" (Matthew 24:37–39). White (1900) over a century ago stated, similarly, to contemporaries today: Men are rushing on in the chase for gain and selfish indulgence as if there were no God, no heaven, and no hereafter. In Noah's day, the warning of the flood was sent to startle men in their wickedness and call them to repentance. So, the message of Christ's soon coming is designed to arouse men from their absorption in worldly things. It is intended to awaken them to a sense of eternal realities, that they may give heed to the invitation to the Lord's table (p. 228).

The gospel as proclaimed by the third angel is ennobling and liberating. In Luke 4:16–19, Jesus announces His mission and work for the entire world: "And He came to Nazareth, where He had been brought up, and as His custom was, He went into the synagogue on the Sabbath day, and stood up for to read. And there was delivered unto Him the book of Esias. And when He had opened the book, He found the place where it was written: "The spirit of the Lord is upon Me, because He hath anointed me to preach the gospel to the poor: He hath sent Me to heal the broken-hearted, to preach deliverance to the captives, and recovering of sight to the blind, to set at liberty them that are bruised, to preach the acceptable year of the Lord." Christ Himself became our ransom, and liberator from the oppressive power of Satan. "Ye are not your own," He says, "for ye are bought with a price." We are bought from a power whose slaves we were. The price our ransom cost was the only begotten Son of God. His blood alone could ransom guilty man. "For God so loved the world that He gave His only begotten Son that whosoever believes in Him, should have everlasting life" (White 1926).

As stated earlier in this chapter, the 1890s was the decade of repeated appeals from the pen of Ellen G. White to the church, urging its evangelistic forces to enter the great harvest field of the South. Her son accepted the challenge. Although he sometimes opposed his parents' rules in the home and often pushed the limits of restraints, he had a personality that God could use for the heroic venture to the dangerous elements in the South and minister to slaves. In a letter to him Mrs. White wrote:

Dear Son Edson,

In answer to your question as to whether it would be well to fit up your steamer *Morning Star*, to be used for the conveyance of missionary workers to places that otherwise they could not reach, I will say that I have been shown how, when you first went to the Southern field, you used this boat as your home, and as a place on which to receive those interested in the truth. The novelty of the idea excited curiosity, and many came to see and hear. I know that, through the agency of this boat, places have been reached where till then the light of truth had never shone,—places represented to me as "the hedges." *Morning Star* has been instrumental in sowing the seeds of truth in many hearts, and there are those who have first seen the light of truth while on this boat. On it angel feet have trodden. Yet I would have you consider the dangers as well as the advantages of this line of work. The greatest caution will need to be exercised by all who enter the Southern field. They must not trust to unchristian feelings or prejudices. The truth is to be proclaimed. Christ is to be uplifted as the Savior of mankind. Unless men of extreme caution are chosen as leaders and burden-bearers, men who trust in the Lord, knowing that they will be kept by His power, the efforts of the workers will be in vain. The brethren are to consider these things, and then move forward in faith.

One thing I urge upon you: the necessity of counselling with your brethren. There are those who will feel that anything you may have to do with boats is a snare; but, my son, if there is a class of people in out-of-way places who can be reached only by means of boats, talk the matter over with your brethren. Pray earnestly regarding it, and the Spirit of God will point out the way. I see no reason why a boat should not be utilized as a means of bringing to those in darkness the light of Him who is "the bright and morning Star" (White 1903).

As a result of Edson's mission work in the South, thousands of souls have been saved and a historical Black college/university (HBCU) named Oakwood Industrial School was established in 1896 in Huntsville, Alabama. It has been perpetuating Edson's mission since its inception. As the work rapidly accelerated throughout the South, Black congregations were established. In 1886 Edgefield Junction, Tennessee, became the location of the first Black SDA church. The pastor was Harry Lowe, formerly a Baptist minister. The second Black SDA congregation was established in Louisville, Kentucky, in 1890, with A. Barry as its pastor. The third Black SDA church was started in Bowling Green, Kentucky, in 1891, followed by churches in New Orleans, Louisiana, in 1892 (started by Charles Kinney), and another church started in Nashville, Tennessee, in 1894. The Edgefield Junction, Louisville, Bowling Green, and Nashville churches are located in what is now the South Central Conference, which is stationed in Nashville, Tennessee, and the New Orleans church is located in what is now the Southwest Region Conference, and is situated in Dallas, Texas.

Oakwood Industrial School renamed Oakwood College in 1943 and given the name Oakwood University in 2008. Initially, it had only four buildings on campus, four teachers, and 16 students (eight women and eight men). The institution, with a property value of about $10,000 at that time, began in response to the appeals of Edson White and his mother, Ellen White. This institution was pivotal to the development of Black leaders and was a training center for evangelistic work in the South. General Conference leaders purchased a 360-acre farm (the property later included 1,000 acres) about five miles north of Huntsville, Alabama. Ellen White identified this as a place that God had selected and would richly bless. She visited the campus in 1904, and through the remaining years of her life she constantly promoted and supported the school. On numerous occasions she spoke of having received "divine instruction" in regard to Oakwood College. It has been estimated that 85 percent of the Black leaders of the church have spent some time at Oakwood College during their educational experience (Baker, 2020).

From Noah's ark to the *Morning Star* there has been seamless liberating missions to save human beings from impending bondage and eternal destruction. Oakwood University serves efficaciously in this capacity. It is a great gift that keeps on producing great mission driven leaders that impact not only African Americans, but the world. Despite the fragility of the United States' Constitution and looming signs of the imminent return of Jesus may God help each of us to lead lives that promote freedom of conscience, liberty, and justice for all until time shall be no longer.

Daniel prophesized that at the end of time amidst persecution by the government and its attempt to coerce inhabitants to receive the Mark of the Beast or to do slave labor, the Bright and *Morning Star* will stand for the children of the people. "And at that time shall Michael stand up, the great prince which stands for the children of thy people: and there shall be a time of trouble, such as never was since there was a nation even to that same time: and at that time thy people shall be delivered, every one that shall be found written in the book" (Daniel 12:1).

John the prophet wrote, "And I said unto him, Sir, thou knowest. And he said to me, These are they which came out of great tribulation, and have washed their robes, and made them white in the blood of the Lamb. Therefore are they before the throne of God and serve him day and night in his temple: and he that sitteth on the throne shall dwell among them. They shall hunger no more, neither thirst anymore; neither shall the sun light on them, nor any heat. For the Lamb which is in the midst of the throne shall feed them and shall lead them unto living fountains of waters: and God shall wipe away all tears from their eyes." "And there shall be no more death, neither sorrow, nor crying, neither shall there be any more pain: for the former things are passed away" (Revelation 7:14–17; Revelation 21:4).

REFERENCES

Allen, Francis, William Ware, Pickard Charles, and Garrison, McKim Lucy (. 1867). Slave Songs of the United States, p. xl

Andrews, J. N. 1851. "Thoughts on Revelation XIII and XIV." *Review and Herald*, Vol. 1(11), 82–84.

Apostate Protestantism Will Form the Image to the Beast, https://www.costministries.com/picture-studies/for-sdas/apostate- protestantism-will-form-the-image-to-the-beast/.

The American Civil War: americaslegacylinks.com Shcraft, Chris. Creation History Our Story.
Webpage: http://mail.nwcreation.net/nwinfo.html

Delbert Baker: Black Seventh day Adventists and the influence of Ellen G. White, January 2020.
https://library.mibckerala.org/lms_frame/eBook/Perspective2.pdf

Bradford, William, Paget, Valerian. 2015. *History of the Plymouth Settlement 1608–1650*. Creative Media Partners, LLC.

British Library. Timelines: Sources from History.

Brown, Deneen. 2020. *National Geographic*: nationalgeographic.com.

Cartwright, M. J. 1889. "Old Ship Of Zion." in *The Gospel Pilot Hymnal*,
    edited by Daniel Towner & French E. Oliver (Chicago, Illinois:
    Towner & Oliver, 1889), number 140.
    http://www.hymntime.com/tch/htm/o/l/d/s/oldshipz.htm.

Cartwright, S March 12, 1851, Reported to the Medical Association of
    Louisiana:
    https://www.washingtonpost.com/local/a-brief-
    history-of-the-enduring-phony-science-that-perpetuates-
    white-supremacy/2019/04/29/20e6aef0-5aeb-11e9-a00e-
    050dc7b82693_story.html

Cassidy, Richard J., John's Gospel in New Perspective: Christology and
    the Realities of Roman Power. With the New Essay Johannine
    Foot-washing and Roman Slavery, Eugene OR: WIPF& Stock,
    2015, pp.119–123.

Citizens Commission on Human Rights of Colorado 2018, CCHR CO
    Posted on June 19, 2021. Tags American Psychiatric Association,
    APA, Benjamin Rush, human rights, racism, scientific racism,
    slave https://psychiatricfraud.org/tag/benjamin-rush/.

Douglass, Frederick, The New National Era, August 17, 1871, recalling
    the Atlantic slave Trade.

Edson, Hiram. 1850. Case to J. White (Case, November 1850, No. 11, p.
    85). Joseph Bates, August 5, 1851, Vol. 2, No. 1, pp. 3-4; Nichols,
    September 2, 1851, Vol. 2, No. 3, p. 22.

Elwell, Walter. 1996. *Baker's Evangelical Dictionary of Biblical Theology.* Published by Baker's Books, a division of Baker Book House Company, Grand Rapid, Michigan.

Epstein, Dena. 2003. *Sinful Tunes and Spirituals: Black Folk Music of the Civil War.* University of Illinois Press. p. 290.

Ezebuiro, Peace. 2021. Eight Most Horrific and Inhuman Black Slaves Punishment in The History Of Slavery November 3, 2021, answersafrica.com.

Frazier, Justin. 2022. "Why the *Mayflower* Matters 400 Years Later." https://rcg.org/realtruth/articles/201026-001.html.

Gospel Music Lyrics, 12/14/2007 https://gospelyrics.blogspot.com/2007/12/old-ship-of-zion.html.

Graybill, Ron. 1971. *Mission to Black America: The True Story of James Edson White and the Riverboat* Morning Star.

Harper, Kyle. 2011. *Slavery in the Late Roman World, AD 275–425.* Cambridge University Press, 2011, pp 58–60, and footnote 150.

James Kendall Hosmer, LL. D., ed. Original Narratives of Early American History: Winthrop's Journals "History of New England," 1630-1649. Volume I. New York: Charles Scribner's Sons, 1908. Pages 187, 260, 331. Google Books.

Jackson, Vanessa. 2015. "In Our Own Voices: African American Stories of Oppression, Survival and Recovery in the Mental Health System," pp 1–36, p. 4–8 http://www.mindfreedom.org/mindfreedom/jackson.shtm.

Research on the 1st Century Galilee Boat of the Ancient Galilee Boat https://www.jesusboat.com/the-jesus-boat-research/.

Johnson, Caleb. 2020. http://*Mayflower*history.com/voyage. ellenwhite.org

John Winthrop's Journal 1636, p. 260 https://marbleheadmuseum. org/ship-desire/

Hayes, John, Mandell, Sara. 1998. The Jewish People in Classical Antiquity: From Alexander to Bar Kochba. Westminster John Knox Press, Louisville London Leiden. War 111:562-542. https://www.jesusboat.com/the-jesus-boat-research/.

Kasten, Patricia. The Compass. January 19, 2018, thecompassnews.org. Philibert-Ortega, Gena African American Slave Trade: Ships & Records for Genealogy March 3, 2014. genealogybank.com.

Kinlaw, F. Dennis. 2017. This Day with the Master, November 14.

Loconte, Joseph. 2017. Martin Luther and the Long March to Freedom of Conscience. October 26, 2017. nationalgeographic.com.

Loughborough, J.N. 1858. The Two-horned Beast Revelation 13, The Advent Review and Sabbath Herald, 8 April 1858, 167–168.

Moore, George. 1866. Notes on the History of Slavery in Massachusetts. New York: Appletonand Co., page 6-9 Archive.org.

Nichol, Francia. 1951. Amalgamation. Review and Herald Publishing Association, Washington DC.

NW Creation Network 2022: nwcreation.net.

Odom, Robert L. (1948) The Horns of Revelation 13:11. Ministry International Journal for Pastors. https://www.ministrymagazine.org/archive/1948/07/two-horns-of-revelation-1311

Pilgrim Ship Lists Early 1600's. pakrat-pro.com .

Quant, Brenda, *Desire* Lines: From Slave Ships to the 9the Ward. Traveling the Hidden Paths of History, July 8, 2015.

Rediker, Marcus. 2008. The Slave Ship: A Human History September 30. The Penguin Group. New York, New York.

Review and Herald Publishing Association: https://rhpa.netadventist.org/our-story.

Sawchuk, Stephen. 2021. What Is Critical Race Theory, and Why Is It Under Attack. Education Week May 18, 2021.

Strong's Exhaustive Concordance, Undated Edition KJV. Hendrickson Publishers 2009.

Stern, Jessie and Samson, Rachel. 2021. The Heart and Science of Attachment. Why We Treat Others As We Have Been Treated. Psychology Today, Sussex Publisher, LLC August, 2021.

Steven, Sharry. 2022. Packrat Productions: pakrat-pro.com.

Townsend, in "The New World Compared with the Old."

Uriah Smith. "The Warning Voice of Time and Prophecy," Advent Review and Sabbath Herald, 23 June 1853, 8.

The General Conference Bulletin. April 25, 1901, paragraph 7.

The General Conference Bulletin. April 25, 1901, paragraph 35.

Than, Ker. 2010. "Noah's Ark Found in Turkey," *National Geographic News.*

The Review and Herald February 9, 1892, Paragraph 1.

Tozer, A.W Bible.org.

White, Ellen. 1911. *The Acts of the Apostle.* Mountain View, CA: Pacific Press Publishing Association,

White, Ellen (. 1913). Counsel to Parents, and Students. Pacific Press.

White, Ellen. 1953. Colporteur Ministry. Mountain View, CA: Pacific Press Publishing Association.

White, Ellen. (2002). The DesireDesire of Ages. Pacific Press Publishing Association.

White, Ellen (. 1983). From Eternity Past., Pacific Press Publishing Association.

White, Ellen. 2021. *Counsel for the Church.* Ellenwhite.org.

White, Ellen. 2021. *Early Writings.* Ellenwhite.org.

White, Ellen. 1882. *Early Writings*. Washington, DC: Review and Herald Publishing Association.

White, Ellen. 1903. Selections from the Testimonies for the church For the Study of Those Attending the General Conference in Oakland, CA., March 27, 1903, p. 79.

White, Ellen. 1983. *From Eternity Past*. Pacific Press Publishing Association.

White Ellen. (1976 –1891). The Lonely Years, Volume 3.

White, Ellen. 1888. "Ellen G. White to O. A. Olsen, Letter 127," *The Ellen G. White 1888 Materials*.

White, Ellen. 1888. *The Great Controversy*. Washington, DC: Review and Herald Publishing.

White, Ellen G. Estate. 2003. *The Genealogy of Ellen G. White*. whiteestate.org

White, Ellen. 1901. *The Southern Work*. Review and Harold Publishing Association, Washington, DC.

White, Ellen. 1903. *Education*. Mountain View, CA: Pacific Press Publishing Association.

White, Ellen. 1926. *Testimony Studies on Diet and Foods*. Loma Linda, CA: College of Medical Evangelists.

White, Ellen. 1984. *From Eternity Past*. Shelter Publications.

White, Ellen. 2005. *Slaves and Master*. https://www.ellenwhite.info/slavery-revived.htm.

White, Ellen. Manuscript Releases, vol. 2, p. :299. (p. 276).

White, Ellen. (1899.) Manuscript Release,Vol. 4 Nos. 210--259, p. 12.2 .

White, Ellen. (1895.) Manuscript 22a, 1895. Vol. 10, par 4 .

White, James. 1861. "The Sacredness of Slavery." *Advent Review and Sabbath Herald*, June 11,1861, p. 17.

White, Ellen. 1945. *Spiritual Gifts*. Review and Herald Publishing Association, Washington, DC.

White, Ellen. 1890. *Patriarchs and Prophets*. Review and Herald Publishing Association, Washington, DC.

World Future Fund. 2001. worldfuturefund.org.

White, Ellen. 1984. *From Heaven with Love*. Pacific Publishing Association.

White, Ellen. 1900. *Steps to Christ*. Review and Herald Publishing Association.

APPENDIX

Ellen White's Experiences on Boats

The practice of using boats to travel and to herald the gospel existed long before the *Morning Star*. Perhaps Edson White, the designer of the *Morning Star*, derived some of his ideas for building a mission boat grew out of his exposure to them. From early childhood he accompanied his mother on certain voyages and heard her recount personal encounters with God while on boats. Mrs. White used these vessels for mission work and a range of other purposes. She utilized them to escape the exhausting aspects of ministering to others so that she herself could hear the spirit of God speaking and restoring her spiritual vitality. Engaging in recreational activities when she was fatigued from caring for the people allowed Ellen to unwind. Whenever she felt the need, she took Jesus's advice and came aside for rest. Jesus commanded His disciples of old and His people today to "Come ye yourselves apart ... and rest a while" (Mark 6:31).

Mrs. White enjoyed periods of respite and repose, whether in the mountains, on some lake, or on the open water. In midlife, while she was living near the Pacific Press in Northern California, it was proposed that a day be spent in rest and recreation on the water. She, with her home and office family, were asked to join the publishing house family, and she readily accepted the invitation. Her husband was in the east on denominational business. It is in a letter to him that we find her account of this experience. Mrs. White stated, "after enjoying a wholesome lunch on the beach, the entire group went for a boat ride on San Francisco Bay. The captain of the sailing craft was a member of the church, and it was a pleasant afternoon." Then it was proposed that they go out into the open ocean. In recounting the experience Ellen White wrote:

"The waves ran high, and we were tossed up and down so very grandly. I was highly elevated in my feelings but had no words to say to anyone. It was grand! The spray dashed over us. The wind was strong outside the golden gate, and I never enjoyed anything as much in my life!" (page 26). Then she observed the watchful eyes of the captain and the readiness of the crew to obey his commands, and she commented:

> "God holds the winds in His hands. He controls the waters. We are mere specks upon the broad, deep waters of the Pacific; yet angels of heaven are sent to guard this little sailboat as it races over the waves. Oh, the wonderful works of God! So far beyond our understanding! At one glance He beholds the highest heavens and the midst of the sea!" (White 1876).

Another day was spent on the water, through the courtesy of one of the members of the church in San Francisco, Brother Chittendon, who owned a large sailboat. Ellen White fully enjoyed the occasion. She wrote:

> Brother Chittendon took out a number of us on the water in his boat, Sister Chittendon, Waggoner, Loughborough, and wife, Mary Clough, Edson, Emma, Frank, Willie Jones, Bro. O. B. Jones, Charles

Jones, myself and the little girls. We remained on the water and beach all day. Sailed out of the Golden Gate upon the ocean. There was no wind to take us out of the harbor. Charlie employed a steam tug to take us out. One of his friends managed the steamboat. Mary and Emma were seasick. I was not sick at all. The waves ran high, and we were tossed up and down so very grandly. I was highly elevated in my feelings but had no words to say to anyone. It was grand. The spray dashing over us. The watchful captain giving his orders, the ready hands to obey. The wind was blowing strong, and I never enjoyed anything so much in my life.

Ellen continued, "I was today to write upon Christ walking on the sea and stilling the tempest. Oh, how this scene was impressed upon my mind. Brother Chittendon says Sister White looks just happy, but she does not say a word to anyone. I was filled with awe with my own thoughts. Everything seemed so grand in that ocean, the waves running so high. The majesty of God and His works occupied my thoughts. He holds the winds in His hand, He controls the waters. Finite beings mere specks upon the broad deep waters of the Pacific were we in the sight of God, yet angels of heaven were sent from His excellent glory to guard that little sailboat that was careening over the waves. Oh, the wonderful works of God! So much above our comprehension! He at one glance beholds the highest heavens and the midst of the sea. "How vividly before my mind was the boat with the disciples buffeting the waves. … I am glad I went upon the water. I can write better than before" (Letter 5, 1876).

In addition to recreational activities, that provided needed rejuvenation, God gave Mrs. White a vision while onboard a boat. Amazingly, this event transpired during a storm, which shows that God never takes His watchful eye from His chosen ones. He promised: "I will instruct you and teach you in the way you should go; I will guide you with My eye" (Psalm 32:8).

ELLEN WHITE'S VISION ON THE WATER

In 1846, while at Fairhaven, Massachusetts, Mrs. White wrote the following:

> My sister (who usually accompanied me at that time), Sister A., Brother G., and myself started in a sailboat to visit a family on West's Island. It was almost night when we started. We had gone but a short distance when a storm suddenly arose. It thundered and lightened, and the rain came in torrents upon us. It seemed plain that we must be lost, unless God should deliver. I knelt in the boat and began to cry to God to deliver us. And there upon the tossing billows, while the water washed over the top of the boat upon us, I was taken off in vision and saw that sooner would every drop of water in the ocean be dried up than we perish, for my work had but just begun. After I came out of the vision all my fears were gone, and we sang and praised God, and our little boat was to us a floating Bethel. The

editor of The Advent Herald has said that my visions were known to be "the result of mesmeric operations." But, I ask, what opportunity was there for mesmeric operations in such a time as that? Brother G. had more than he could well do to manage the boat. He tried to anchor, but the anchor dragged. Our little boat was tossed upon the waves and driven by the wind, while it was so dark that we could not see from one end of the boat to the other. Soon the anchor held, and Brother G. called for help. There were but two houses on the island, and it proved that we were near one of them, but not the one where we wished to go. All the family had retired to rest except a little child, who providentially heard the call for help upon the water. Her father soon came to our relief, and, in a small boat, took us to the shore. We spent the most of that night in thanksgiving and praise to God for His wonderful goodness unto us (White 2021).

Voyage to Australia

About forty years after Ellen's vision on a boat she embarked on a voyage in which she felt deported into exile. This was the time when the General Conference GC commissioned her to Australia. She was reluctant to go because she was involved in meaningful church activities in America and advocating for slaves in the South. Nevertheless, in obedience to the assignment, she adhered but later expressed her opinion relative to God's leading.

After the GC voted to send Mrs. White to Australia in 1891, she stated that on November 12, about two in the afternoon, "We went on board the steamship S.S. *Alameda*" and set sail (*Review and Herald* 1892). Although she had difficulty adhering to the wish of Elder Olsen, who was the president of GC at the time, and his leaders, she obeyed them. She later wrote:

> I have not, I think, revealed the entire workings that led me here to Australia. Perhaps you may never fully understand the matter. The Lord was not in our leaving America. He did not reveal that it was his will that I should leave Battle Creek. The Lord did not plan this, but he let you all move after your own imaginings. The Lord would have had William C. White, his mother, and her workers remain in America. We were needed at the heart of the work, and had your spiritual perception discerned the true situation, you would never have consented to the movements made. But the Lord read the hearts of all. There was so great a willingness to have us leave, that the Lord permitted this thing to take place. Those who were weary of the testimonies borne were left without the persons who bore them. Our separation from Battle Creek was to let men have their own will and way, which they thought superior to the way of the Lord (Ellen G. White to O. A. Olsen, Letter 127).

Despite Ellen's perception of the apparent ill will of GC leadership, her voice would not be silenced, and her passion would not be quenched regarding the need for the church to evangelize people of color (called "colored people" at the time). Her burden for the work of liberating the colored people in the south seemed even greater. Before she was sent to Australia, she tenaciously urged the leaders of GC of the church's duty to the colored people. This decision could have silence her voice, but to no avail. Even while she was residing in Australia, the 1890s was the decade of repeated appeals from her pen to the church, urging its evangelistic forces to enter the great harvest field of the South. First appeared the far-reaching Testimony to Church Leaders in 1891, headed "Our Duty to the Colored People." This document was circulated in manuscript form and then printed in a leaflet. It was this that stirred the missionary zeal of Ellen White's son James Edson White and led him to launch evangelistic and educational work among the neglected people of the South. In doing this he built a missionary boat christened "The *Morning Star*", which provided residence, chapel, schoolroom, and printing office. Evangelistic work started at Vicksburg, Mississippi, in January 1895. Ten articles written by Ellen G. White for publication in the Review and Herald soon supplemented the basic appeal of 1891. These were published in 1895 and 1896 while Mrs. White was living in Australia.

Printed in the United States
by Baker & Taylor Publisher Services